SNACKS AND REFRESHMENTS

Better Homes and Gardens

PRINTED IN THE UNITED STATES OF AMERICA. FIRST EDITION. NINTH PRINTING, 1972.

LIBRARY OF CONGRESS CATALOG CARD NUMBER: 63-4079

SBN: 696-01006-2

Grilled Cheese Italiano

Sombrero Spread, Tostadas

Ribbon Alaska Pie—a dessert dazzler!

Grand Glorious Punch

Contents

This seal means recipe goodness!

Every recipe in this book is *endorsed* by Better Homes & Gardens Test Kitchen. Each food was tested over and over till it rated superior— in practicality, ease of preparation, and deliciousness.

Better Homes *and Gardens*
TEST KITCHEN

Put on a party with ease. Guests chef their own skewers, munch on tasty nibbles from this chapter.

Dips, spreads, and snacks

Zippy dips and dunks

Blue-cheese Dunk

4 ounces blue cheese, crumbled
(about 1 cup)
1 3-ounce package cream cheese,
softened
2 tablespoons milk
2 tablespoons salad dressing

Combine ingredients; beat with electric mixer till light and fluffy; or use electric blender. Sprinkle with snipped parsley. For dippers, serve celery, carrot sticks, cauliflowerets, or cherry tomatoes—see page 7.

Three-cheese Dip

¼ cup water
1 cup cream-style cottage cheese
• • •
2 3-ounce packages cream cheese,
softened
2 tablespoons crumbled blue cheese
1 small clove garlic
Few drops bottled hot pepper sauce

Pour water into electric blender. Add cottage cheese; cover and blend at high speed about 20 seconds. Stop motor. Add remaining ingredients. Cover; blend 30 seconds or till smooth. Makes about 2 cups.

Dieters' Cottage Dip

In electric blender or mixer, place one 12-ounce carton (1½ cups) cream-style cottage cheese, 1 tablespoon mayonnaise or salad dressing, and 1 teaspoon salad-spice-and-herb mix. Blend till almost smooth. Chill. Sprinkle with parsley. Pass celery and carrot sticks. Makes 1½ cups.

1-2-3 Dip

1 cup dairy sour cream
½ envelope cheese-garlic flavored
salad-dressing mix
¼ teaspoon salt
Few drops bottled hot pepper sauce

Combine ingredients. Chill.

Hearty Clam Delight

2 3-ounce packages cream cheese
2 teaspoons lemon juice
2 teaspoons grated onion
1 teaspoon Worcestershire sauce
3 or 4 drops bottled hot pepper sauce
¼ teaspoon salt
• • •
1 7- or 7½-ounce can (about 1 cup)
minced clams, chilled and drained
1 tablespoon minced parsley

Stir cream cheese to soften. Add lemon juice, onion, Worcestershire, hot pepper sauce, and salt. Beat with rotary or electric beater till light and fluffy, or use electric blender. Stir in clams and parsley. Serve with crackers or chips and crisp relishes. Makes about 1½ cups.

Anchovy-Olive Dip

1 cup dairy sour cream
½ cup finely chopped stuffed
green olives
1½ tablespoons anchovy paste
½ teaspoon grated onion

Combine ingredients; mix well. Chill.

Crab-Cheese Special

1 8-ounce package cream cheese,
softened
¼ cup light cream or milk
• • •
2 teaspoons lemon juice
1½ teaspoons Worcestershire sauce
1 clove garlic, minced
Dash salt and pepper
1 6½- or 7½-ounce can (1 cup)
crab meat, drained

Beat cream cheese, gradually adding cream; beat till smooth.

Add lemon juice, Worcestershire sauce, garlic, salt, and pepper. Remove bony bits from crab; snip meat in fine pieces and stir into cream-cheese mixture. Chill. Makes about 1½ cups dip.

*Scoop into fluffy
Guacamole—a favorite
from south of the border!*

Guacamole

  2 ripe avocados, mashed (2 cups)
  1 tablespoon minced onion
  1 clove garlic, minced
  ¼ teaspoon chili powder
  ¼ teaspoon salt
  Dash pepper

  • • •

  ⅓ cup mayonnaise
  6 slices crisp-cooked bacon, crumbled

Combine mashed avocado, onion, garlic, and seasonings in small bowl. Spread top with mayonnaise, sealing to edges of bowl; chill.

   To serve, stir in the mayonnaise and bacon. Top with additional crumbled bacon. Pass with corn chips. Makes about 2 cups.

   Note: The mayonnaise "coat" over the top helps keep avocado bright.

Creamy Braunschweiger Dip

  ½ pound (1 cup) Braunschweiger
  1 cup dairy sour cream
  1 envelope onion-soup mix
  1 teaspoon Worcestershire sauce
  Few drops bottled hot pepper sauce

Combine ingredients; chill till serving time.

Smoky Egg Dip

  6 hard-cooked eggs, sieved
  ⅓ cup mayonnaise
  1 tablespoon soft butter or margarine
  ½ teaspoon salt
  2 teaspoons prepared mustard
  1½ teaspoons lemon juice
  1½ teaspoons Worcestershire sauce
  ⅛ teaspoon liquid smoke
  2 drops bottled hot pepper sauce
  Dash pepper
  4 slices crisp-cooked bacon,
     crumbled (optional)

Combine ingredients except bacon. Beat till smooth. Chill. At serving time, fold in crumbled bacon, reserving a little for trim *or*, omit bacon, sprinkle with paprika. Serve with crisp crackers. Makes 1¾ cups.

Deviled-ham Dunk

  1 5-ounce jar pimento-cheese spread
  1 2¼-ounce can deviled ham
  ½ cup mayonnaise or salad dressing
  1 tablespoon minced onion
  Few drops bottled hot pepper sauce

Combine ingredients; chill. Sprinkle with snipped parsley. Makes about 1⅓ cups.

Hot dips

Sombrero Spread

A dandy bean snack, Mexican style. Like flavor "fire"? Add more chili powder to taste—

½ pound ground beef
¼ cup chopped onion
¼ cup extra-hot catsup
1½ teaspoons chili powder
½ teaspoon salt
1 8-ounce can (1 cup) red kidney
    beans (with liquid)
. . .
½ cup shredded sharp process
    American cheese
¼ cup chopped stuffed green olives
¼ cup chopped onion
1 recipe Mexican Tostadas

Brown meat and ¼ cup onion in skillet or chafing dish. Stir in catsup, chili powder, and salt. Mash in beans. Heat through.

Garnish with the cheese, olives, and ¼ cup onion, as shown on frontispiece. Makes 1½ cups. Serve hot as a spread for Mexican Tostadas, or for corn chips.

Mexican Tostadas

Start with fresh, frozen, or canned tortillas. (If tortillas are frozen, thaw.) Cut each tortilla in quarters. Fry in shallow hot fat about 4 minutes, turning once. Drain on paper towels.

Sweet-'n-Sour Wiener Bites

The hot "dip" is mustard and currant jelly—

1 6-ounce jar (¾ cup) prepared
    mustard
1 10-ounce jar (1 cup) currant jelly
. . .
1 pound (8 to 10) frankfurters, canned
    Vienna sausages, or cocktail wieners

Mix mustard and jelly in chafing dish or double boiler. Diagonally slice frankfurters in bite-size pieces. (Cut Vienna sausages or cocktail wieners in half.) Add to sauce and heat through. Makes 8 servings.

Sour Cream-Cheese Dip

1 can condensed bean with bacon soup
1 6-ounce roll garlic-flavored cheese
    food, diced
. . .
1 cup dairy sour cream
¼ cup minced onion
¼ teaspoon bottled hot pepper sauce
Chili powder

In saucepan or chafing dish, combine soup and cheese. Heat, stirring constantly, till cheese melts. Stir in sour cream, onion, and hot pepper sauce. Heat through.

Dash with chili powder. Pass with chips and crackers. Makes 2⅔ cups.

Mexican Bean Dip

A he-man appetizer! For speed, use a blender to sieve the pork and beans—

1 No. 2½ can (3½ cups) pork and
    beans in tomato sauce, sieved
½ cup shredded sharp process
    American cheese
1 teaspoon garlic salt
1 teaspoon chili powder
½ teaspoon salt
Dash cayenne pepper
2 teaspoons vinegar
2 teaspoons Worcestershire sauce
½ teaspoon liquid smoke
. . .
4 slices crisp-cooked bacon, crumbled

Combine all ingredients except bacon; heat in chafing dish or double boiler. Top with crumbled bacon. Serve with corn chips or potato chips. Makes 3 cups.

Easy Cheese Dunk

½ can condensed cream of
    mushroom soup
2 6-ounce rolls garlic-flavored
    cheese food, cut up
1 teaspoon Worcestershire sauce
⅛ to ¼ teaspoon bottled hot
    pepper sauce
3 tablespoons cooking sherry

In saucepan or chafing dish, combine soup and cheese food. Heat over very low heat till cheese melts, stirring often to blend. Add remaining ingredients. Keep hot for dipping. Makes about 2 cups.

Company Clam Dip

1 6½- or 7½-ounce can
   minced clams
2 tablespoons minced onion
2 tablespoons butter or margarine
1 tablespoon catsup
Few drops bottled hot pepper sauce
1 cup diced sharp process
   American cheese
2 tablespoons chopped
   pitted ripe olives
1 teaspoon Worcestershire sauce

Drain clams, reserving 1 tablespoon of the liquor. Cook onion in butter till tender but not brown; add clams, reserved clam liquor, and remaining ingredients. Heat till cheese melts and mixture is hot. Makes 1¼ cups. Serve with crackers and chips.

Lobster Dip Elegante

1 8-ounce package cream cheese
¼ cup mayonnaise or salad dressing
1 clove garlic, crushed
1 teaspoon grated onion
1 teaspoon prepared mustard
1 teaspoon sugar
Dash seasoned salt

• • •

1 5-ounce can (about 1 cup) lobster,
   flaked
3 tablespoons cooking sauterne

Melt cream cheese over low heat, stirring constantly. Blend in mayonnaise, garlic, onion, mustard, sugar, and salt. Stir in lobster and cooking sauterne; heat through. Makes about 1¾ cups. Serve hot with Melba toast and assorted crackers.

Company Clam Dip—your guests won't be able to stop nibbling!

Olive-Cheese Ball

One of the best cracker spreads ever! This nibblers' special is a delightful combination of blue cheese, cream cheese, and ripe olives. You can count on it to be a favorite with the men!

Simply superb spreads

Olive-Cheese Ball

1 8-ounce package cream cheese, softened
8 ounces blue cheese, crumbled
¼ cup soft butter or margarine
⅔ cup well-drained chopped ripe olives (1 4½-ounce can)
1 tablespoon minced chives

. . .

⅓ cup chopped California walnuts or toasted diced almonds

Blend cheeses and butter. Stir in olives and chives. Chill slightly for easier shaping. Form in ball on serving dish. Chill thoroughly. Just before serving, sprinkle nuts over ball. Trim with parsley. Serve with assorted crackers. Makes 3 cups.

Three-cheese Spread

Thoroughly combine ½ pound sharp Cheddar cheese, shredded (2 cups), with 4 ounces blue cheese, crumbled, and one 3-ounce package cream cheese, softened. Serve with crackers. Makes about 2 cups.

Cheese-Pecan Ball

An easy snack—it's cream cheese spiked with bottled steak sauce. Pecans add crunch—

1 8-ounce package cream cheese, softened
1 to 2 tablespoons bottled steak sauce
1 cup pecans, finely chopped
1 clove garlic, minced
Few drops bottled hot pepper sauce

. . .

Chopped parsley
Paprika

With beater or spoon, combine cream cheese, steak sauce, nuts, garlic, and hot pepper sauce. Form in ball; wrap in waxed paper; chill several hours or till firm.

Unwrap ball and place on serving dish. Sprinkle parsley to make strip about 1 inch wide down center of ball. Sprinkle both sides with paprika. Keep chilled; remove from refrigerator about 15 minutes before serving. Serve as a spread with assorted crackers. Makes 1½ cups.

Braunschweiger Glace

Delicious "pate" in a shimmery jacket of jellied consomme. See it on the cover—

1 envelope (1 tablespoon) unflavored
    gelatin
½ cup cold water
1 can condensed consomme
½ pound (1 cup) Braunschweiger
3 tablespoons mayonnaise
1 tablespoon vinegar
1 tablespoon minced onion

Soften gelatin in cold water. Heat consomme to boiling. Remove from heat; add gelatin and stir till dissolved. Pour into 2-cup mold; chill till firm. Blend remaining ingredients. Spoon out center of jellied consomme, leaving ½ inch on all sides. Fill center with Braunschweiger mixture. Heat the spooned-out consomme till melted; pour over Braunschweiger. Chill firm.

Unmold. Trim with sprigs of water cress. Offer spreaders. Serve with crackers.

Mock Pate de Foie Gras

½ pound calves' liver
⅓ cup salad oil
2 tablespoons minced parsley
1 tablespoon minced onion
1 tablespoon lemon juice
1 teaspoon Worcestershire sauce

Simmer liver in water to cover for 25 minutes or till done. Put through finest blade of food chopper. Add remaining ingredients. Mix thoroughly. Cover; chill. Makes 1 cup. Serve with crisp crackers.

Appetizer Ham Ball

2 4½-ounce cans deviled ham
3 tablespoons chopped stuffed green
    olives
1 tablespoon prepared mustard
Bottled hot pepper sauce to taste
1 3-ounce package cream cheese,
    softened
2 teaspoons milk

Blend deviled ham, olives, mustard, and hot pepper sauce. Form in ball on serving dish; chill. Combine cream cheese and milk; frost ball with mixture. Chill; remove from refrigerator 15 minutes before serving. Trim with parsley. Pass crackers.

Dried-beef Log

1 8-ounce package cream cheese,
    softened
¼ cup grated Parmesan cheese
1 tablespoon prepared horseradish
⅓ cup chopped stuffed green olives
• • •
2½ ounces (1 cup) dried beef,
    finely snipped

Blend together cream cheese, Parmesan cheese, and horseradish; stir in olives.

On waxed paper, shape in two 6-inch rolls, 1½ inches in diameter. Chill several hours or overnight. Roll each "log" in snipped dried beef. Place on serving plate; offer spreaders; pass assorted crackers.

Dried-beef Canapes

1 teaspoon minced onion
1 tablespoon butter or margarine
2½ ounces (about 1 cup) dried beef,
    finely chopped
1 3-ounce package cream cheese
• • •
Saltines or crisp rye wafers

Cook onion in butter till tender; add dried beef and cook till beef is slightly crisp. Add beef mixture to the cream cheese; blend. Spread on saltines or crisp rye wafers.

Edam Cheese Spread

Have 1 round Edam or Gouda cheese at room temperature. Cut slice off top of cheese. Scoop out center leaving ¼-inch wall. Scallop edge of cheese shell, using a biscuit cutter as guide. Whip cheese with electric mixer. Beat in enough light cream to make spreading consistency. Mound in shell. Serve at room temperature.

Chicken Canapes

1 5-ounce can chicken spread
2 teaspoons mayonnaise
½ cup chopped toasted salted almonds
2 tablespoons sweet-pickle relish
Crisp crackers
Tiny cutouts of canned jellied
    cranberry sauce

Combine first four ingredients. Spread on crackers. Trim with cranberry cutouts.

Know your cheese!

Gourmet's delight — a wonderful array of cheeses, served with fresh fruit!

1 Provolone (salami-style)
2 Longhorn
3 Midget Cheddar (sharp)
4 Gorgonzola
5 Parmesan
6 Edam
7 Cheddar (sharp)
8 Cheddar (soft)
9 Port du Salut
10 Provolone
11 Smoked Swiss
12 Cheddar (medium-sharp)
13 Swiss
14 Roquefort
15 Cheshire

16 Sapsago
17 Stilton
18 Gourmandise
19 Sharp Cheddar spread
20 Cheddar (sliced)
21 Pimento cream-cheese dip
22 Bel Paese
23 Grape cheese
24 Bondost
25 Bondost with caraway seed
26 Christian IX (Danish spiced)
27 Herkimer (a cheddar type)
28 Sage

From around-the-world, cheeses yours to choose!

Cheese	*How it looks and tastes*	*To serve as snack*
Blue, Gorgonzola, Roquefort	Compact, creamy cheeses veined with blue or blue-green mold. Sometimes crumbly. Peppery to sharp piquant flavor. (*Stilton* is similar, but like a blue-veined Cheddar.)	Crumble in dips. Delicious with crackers, fresh pears.
Brick	Medium firm; creamy yellow color, tiny holes. Flavor very mild to medium sharp.	Serve on an appetizer tray. Slices neatly for snack tray or sandwich.
Brie (*bree*)	Similar to Camembert, but slightly firmer. Distinctive sharp flavor, pronounced odor.	Serve same as Camembert. Eat the crust.
Camembert (*kam'-em-bear*)	Creamy yellow inside, with a crust you can eat. When ripe, is consistency of thick cream. Full, rich, mildly pungent flavor.	Serve at room temperature with fruit, crackers. Also nice on an appetizer tray.
Chantelle	Pale yellow with red coat. Mellow: semisoft.	For cheese tray, sandwiches, or dessert.
Cheddar (American)	Favorite all-round cheese. Flavor varies from mild to sharp. Color ranges from natural to yellow-orange; texture from firm to crumbly.	Slice a wedge, serve on snack tray with fruit or crackers. Or, cube, thread on appetizer kabobs with diced ham or olives; shred, use in hot cheese breads.
Cream	Very mild-flavored soft cheese with buttery texture. Rich and smooth. Available plain, whipped. May be flavored for use as spread.	Adds richness and body to dips, sliced or rolled spreads. Or serve with split toasted buttered bagels; pass marmalade.
Edam Gouda	Round, red-coated cheeses; creamy yellow to yellow-orange inside; firm and smooth. Mild nutlike flavor.	Bright hub for snack tray. May be hollowed-out, filled with cheese spread. Or, cut in wedges, pass crackers.
Gjetost (*yeet-ost*)	A sweetish caramel-flavored and -colored cheese, made all or partially from goat's milk. Has a firm, buttery texture.	Delicious with dark breads or crisp crackers.
Liederkranz	Cousin to Limburger, but milder, golden.	Spread on pumpernickel, rye, or crackers.
Limburger	Prized for its robust flavor. When ripened, it's soft and smooth inside, creamy white.	Men like it on dark bread with salty pretzels, coffee. Serve at room temperature.
Mozzarella, Scamorze	Unripened. Mild-flavored and slightly firm. Creamy white to pale yellow.	Cooking cheese. A "must" for miniature pizzas. Good on other hot snacks and in snack-style toasted cheese sandwiches.
Muenster (*mun'-stir*)	Similar to Brick cheese. Mild to mellow flavor, creamy white. Medium hard, tiny holes.	Serve slices on a snack tray.
Parmesan, Romano	Sharp, piquant, very hard cheeses. Come in shakers grated. (Parmesan is also available shredded.) Or grate your own.	Sprinkle on pizza, hot breads, buttered popcorn.
Port du Salut (*por-doo-sa-loo*)	Semisoft, smooth, and buttery. Mild to mellow flavor. Creamy yellow with tiny holes.	Delicious with fresh fruit.
Provolone (*pro-vo-low'-nee*)	A smoked cheese, mellow to sharp flavored. Firm; creamy white. Pear or sausage shaped.	Cut wedges or slices, serve on snack tray.
Swiss	Firm, pale yellow cheese, with large round holes. Nutlike flavor.	Nice choice for ham-cheese tidbits on picks, or for dainty sandwiches. Basic to cheese fondue.
Process cheeses	Cheddar, Brick, Swiss, or Limburger, etc., is melted, pasteurized, and packaged. Result is a smooth, creamy cheese that melts easily. May be flavored with bacon, pimiento, etc.	Melt atop snack-size burgers. Or serve on the snack tray.
Cheese spreads	Delightful blends in favorite cheese flavors, ready to spread. Mild to very sharp. May be smoky, or flavored with clams, relish, etc.	Perfect snacks—many can be served right in the container. Pass crackers.

Hot off the broiler for this snack parade: Pineapple-Bacon Cubes, on picks; Lobster Canapes, and dainty Cheese Pinwheels. High-hat Cheese Puffs pop out of oven—hot dip and dipper rolled into one!

Toasty Braunschweiger Sandwiches give big flavor return for little effort. Spear with stuffed green olives or tiny cocktail onions. Blue-cheese Biscuits are zesty cut-ups from a refrigerated package.

Sizzling snacks

Toasty Braunschweiger Sandwiches

Butter slices of tiny "icebox" rye; sprinkle half the slices with finely chopped onion. Spread Braunschweiger over onion. Top with remaining slices; cut sandwiches in half.

Broil 1½ minutes on each side or till toasted. To serve, anchor with cocktail picks topped with olives or cocktail onions.

Cheese Puffs

12 2-inch bread rounds
¼ cup mayonnaise
½ package (1 packet)
    onion-dip mix
2 tablespoons grated Parmesan
    cheese
1 stiff-beaten egg white

Toast bread rounds on one side in broiler. Blend mayonnaise, dip mix, cheese. Fold in egg white. Spoon onto untoasted sides of bread rounds. Bake at 450° about 10 minutes.

Cheese Pinwheels

Unsliced sandwich loaf
½ pound sharp process cheese,
    shredded (2 cups)
½ cup salad dressing
2 teaspoons lemon juice
2 teaspoons prepared mustard
1 teaspoon salt

Trim crusts from bread. Cut bread in lengthwise slices ¼ inch thick. Combine remaining ingredients. Spread bread slices with cheese mixture. Roll each as for jellyroll, beginning at narrow end. Wrap in foil, chill. Cut in ¼- to ½-inch slices. Broil about 2 minutes. Makes about 56.

Pineapple-Bacon Cubes

Cut bacon slices in half and partially cook; drain. Wrap piece of bacon around a canned pineapple chunk; tack with wood cocktail pick or toothpick. Broil, turning, till bacon is crisp. Serve hot.

Lobster Canapes

2½ dozen 2-inch bread rounds, cut from thinly sliced bread
Salad oil

. . .

1 5-ounce can (about 1 cup) lobster, shredded
½ cup canned condensed cream of mushroom soup
2 tablespoons cooking sherry
1 tablespoon chopped pimiento
¼ teaspoon salt
Few drops bottled hot pepper sauce
¼ cup buttered fine dry bread crumbs

Brush bread rounds lightly with oil; put on cooky sheet. Heat in extremely slow oven (225°) 1¼ to 1½ hours or till dry and crisp.

Combine remaining ingredients except bread crumbs. Spread mixture on the toasted bread rounds. Sprinkle with bread crumbs. Broil 2 to 3 minutes or till crumbs are browned. Serve hot. Makes 30.

Blue-cheese Biscuits

Nippy one-bite breads, quick as a cat's wink—

1 package refrigerated biscuits
¼ cup butter or margarine
3 tablespoons crumbled blue cheese

Cut biscuits in quarters. Arrange in two 8-inch round baking dishes. Melt together butter and cheese; pour mixture over biscuit pieces, being sure to coat them all. Bake in hot oven (400°) about 15 minutes or till golden brown. Serve hot. Makes 40.

Deviled Biscuits

Biscuit bites with deviled ham—good!—

1 package refrigerated biscuits
¼ cup butter or margarine
1 4½-ounce can deviled ham
¼ cup grated Parmesan cheese

Snip biscuits in quarters. Arrange in two 8-inch round baking dishes. Heat together butter and deviled ham, stirring till blended. Pour ham mixture over biscuit pieces, being sure to coat them all. Sprinkle with Parmesan cheese.

Bake in hot oven (400°) about 15 minutes or till golden. Serve hot as snack or as hot bread with a salad supper. Makes 40.

Piccolo Pizzas—a snap to make with a can of refrigerated biscuits!

Brown ½ pound Italian sausage; drain. Add 1 teaspoon crushed oregano; 1 clove garlic, minced. On a greased baking sheet, flatten 10 refrigerated biscuits to 4-inch circles; leave rim. Fill with tomato paste, then sausage.

Sprinkle with 1 cup shredded sharp process cheese, then ¼ cup grated Parmesan. Bake at 425° about 10 minutes.

Swiss Sandwich Puffs

*These are tiny, hot-from-the-broiler canapes.
Filling is spiked with onion—*

16 slices tiny "ice-box" rye bread

. . .

½ cup mayonnaise or salad dressing
¼ cup finely chopped onion
2 tablespoons snipped parsley
8 slices process Swiss cheese

Toast bread on both sides. Combine mayonnaise, onion, and parsley; spread on toast. Cut out rounds of cheese to fit toast; place a cheese round atop each slice, covering mayonnaise mixture.

Broil 3 to 4 inches from heat till cheese is puffy and golden, about 2 to 3 minutes. Trim tops with sliced pitted ripe olives, if desired. Serve hot. Makes 16.

Calico Cuts

Tempting cheese topper on easy-to-fix crust—

1 package hot-roll mix

. . .

1 slightly beaten egg
⅓ cup milk
2 cups (½ pound) shredded sharp
   process American cheese
2 tablespoons chopped canned
   pimiento
½ teaspoon celery seed
Dash pepper

Prepare dough from hot-roll mix and let rise according to package directions.

Divide dough into two parts. Grease fingertips and pat *one piece of dough* evenly into a greased 15½x10½x1-inch jelly-roll pan, shaping a slight rim around edges. Shape *remaining dough* into 6 rolls; place in greased 9x1½-inch pan. Let both rise for 30 to 40 minutes or till double.

Meanwhile, combine egg, milk, cheese, pimiento, celery seed, and pepper. Gently spread this mixture over the dough in the 15½x10½x1-inch pan. Bake in hot oven (425°) for 15 minutes or till golden brown. To serve, cut into 3x2-inch rectangles. Serve hot. Makes about 2 dozen pieces.

Bake rolls in the 9x1½-inch pan in hot oven (400°) for 12 to 15 minutes. Makes ½ dozen rolls.

Snacktime Kabobs

Cut luncheon meat in half lengthwise. Cut each half in about 12 thin lengthwise slices. Thread each strip on skewer in S-shape with a pitted ripe olive and stuffed green olive. Add green pepper squares and cocktail wieners. Brush with melted butter.

Cook over coals till luncheon meat and wieners are browned. Top off kabobs with cherry tomatoes near end of cooking. (See page 6.) Serve with Chili-Butter Sauce. Remember snack plates and forks!

Chili-Butter Sauce: Combine ⅓ cup butter or margarine with 1 cup chili sauce; heat and stir till butter melts. Serve warm.

Tiny Tuna Cream Puffs

½ recipe Cream Puffs, page 47
1 teaspoon instant minced onion
1½ teaspoons lemon juice
1 6½- or 7-ounce can (1 cup) tuna,
   drained and coarsely flaked
½ cup salad dressing or mayonnaise
¾ teaspoon curry powder
1 5-ounce can (⅔ cup) water chestnuts,
   drained and finely chopped

Prepare cream puff mixture. Drop dough by scant teaspoons 2 inches apart on greased baking sheet. Bake at 400° for 20 to 25 minutes. Remove from oven; cool. Split.

Combine onion and lemon juice; let stand 5 minutes. Combine with tuna and remaining ingredients, adding salt and pepper to taste. Fill puffs. To serve, heat on jellyroll pan in hot oven (400°) about 3 minutes or till filling is hot. Makes 60.

Midget Burgers

Toast 10 slices enriched bread on one side. Cut four 1½-inch rounds from each slice. Lightly spread softened butter or margarine on untoasted sides of rounds.

Combine 1 pound ground beef, 2 tablespoons grated onion, 1 tablespoon Worcestershire sauce, and 1 teaspoon salt. Shape mixture in 40 marble-size balls (1 heaping teaspoon each); place one on buttered side of each bread round. Make indentation in center of meat balls.

Broil 4 inches from heat 5 to 6 minutes or till meat is done and edges of bread are toasted. Fill centers with chili sauce (takes ¼ cup). Serve hot. Makes 40.

Teriyaki Kabobs

¾ to 1 pound 1-inch-thick
  sirloin steak
1 13½-ounce can (1⅔ cups)
  pineapple tidbits

· · ·

¼ cup soy sauce
2 tablespoons sugar
1 tablespoon cooking sherry
¼ teaspoon ground ginger *or* ¾
  teaspoon grated fresh gingerroot
1 small clove garlic, minced

Slice meat in strips 3 to 4 inches long, about ⅛ inch thick. Drain pineapple, reserving ¼ cup syrup. In deep bowl, combine reserved syrup with remaining ingredients; mix well. Add meat; stir to coat. Let stand at room temperature 1 hour; stir occasionally.

Lace meat loosely, accordion style, on small skewers, threading pineapple on as you weave in and out. Broil to medium-rare or desired doneness, browning all sides.

Polynesian Rib Kabobs

3 pounds small loin back ribs *or*
  meaty spareribs, sawed in
  2- to 2½-inch strips
¼ cup sugar
1 teaspoon smoked salt
1 recipe Polynesian Barbecue Sauce

Rub spareribs on both sides with sugar and smoked salt; let stand 2 hours. Brush with Polynesian Barbecue Sauce; let stand at least an hour—preferably longer.

Place ribs, meaty side up, on rack in shallow pan. Bake in very hot oven (450°) 15 minutes; spoon off fat. Lower heat control to 350° and continue baking 1 hour or till done, turning ribs and brushing with barbecue sauce a few times. Snip in serving pieces. Pass Chinese Mustard.

Polynesian Barbecue Sauce

½ cup soy sauce
½ cup catsup
3 tablespoons brown sugar
2 to 3 teaspoons grated gingerroot
  or 1 teaspoon ground ginger
1 teaspoon monosodium glutamate

Mix ingredients; let stand overnight before using for Polynesian Rib Kabobs.

Two-way Shrimp Snack

Serve shrimp hot (French-fried), or icy cold, with a trio of delicious sauces. See cover—

French-fried Shrimp:

Peel shell from 2 pounds raw shrimp, leaving last section and tail intact. Cut slit through center back without severing. Open butterfly style; remove black line. Dry shrimp thoroughly; dip in batter.

For batter, combine 1 cup all-purpose flour, ½ teaspoon sugar, ½ teaspoon salt, 1 egg, 1 cup *ice water*, and 2 tablespoons salad oil. Fry shrimp in deep, hot fat (set heat at 400°) till golden brown. Drain. Serve hot with sauces below.

Fresh-cooked Shrimp:

Combine 6 cups water, 2 tablespoons salt, 2 tablespoons vinegar, 2 bay leaves, 1 teaspoon mixed pickling spices, and 2 stalks celery; bring to boiling. Add 2 pounds fresh or frozen shrimp in shells, or peeled and cleaned. Cover, heat to boiling, then lower heat and simmer gently till shrimp turn pink, about 5 minutes. Drain.

If cooked in shell, peel shrimp; remove vein that runs down back. Chill; pass sauces below. Makes 4 to 6 servings.

Red Sauce

Combine 3 tablespoons catsup, 3 tablespoons chili sauce, 1 to 2 tablespoons horseradish, 1 teaspoon lemon juice and dash bottled hot pepper sauce. Serve with French-fried or Fresh-cooked Shrimp.

Caper Sauce

To 1 cup mayonnaise, add ¼ cup drained chopped sour pickles, 1 tablespoon drained chopped capers, and 1½ teaspoons *each* prepared mustard and chopped parsley. Makes 1¼ cups. Serve with French-fried Shrimp or Fresh-cooked Shrimp.

Chinese Mustard

Stir ¼ cup boiling water into ¼ cup dry English mustard. Add ½ teaspoon salt and 2 teaspoons salad oil. If sauce is not yellow enough, add some turmeric.

Pour into serving bowl and sprinkle with parsley. Pass with shrimp (above) or Polynesian Rib Kabobs. Makes ⅓ cup sauce.

Nibbles you can't stop munching

Party Potato Chips

Spread one 4-ounce package potato chips on cooky sheet and sprinkle with ½ cup shredded process American cheese. Sprinkle lightly with thyme, basil, or marjoram. Heat in moderate oven (350°) 5 minutes, or till cheese melts. Serve hot.

Cheese Crisps

1 stick pastry mix
½ cup shredded sharp process
   American cheese
2 tablespoons cold water
. . .
Melted butter or margarine
Poppy seed

Crumble pastry stick, and mix with the cheese. Sprinkle water over, one tablespoon at a time, mixing well with fork till the dough forms a ball. On lightly floured surface, roll very thin in a 12x10-inch rectangle (less than ⅛ inch thick).

Cut in 2-inch squares; brush with butter, sprinkle with poppy seed. Fold each square over in triangle; brush with more butter and sprinkle with more poppy seed; seal edges. Bake on ungreased cooky sheet in very hot oven (450°) about 8 minutes or till lightly browned. Makes about 3 dozen.

Parmesan Rice Squares

2 cups bite-size crisp rice squares
3 tablespoons butter, melted
¼ cup grated Parmesan cheese

In shallow pan, toss rice squares in butter till coated. Sprinkle with Parmesan cheese; toast in slow oven (300°) about 15 minutes, stirring occasionally. Cool.

Scramble

2 pounds mixed salted nuts
1 12-ounce package spoon-size
   shredded-wheat biscuits
1 10½-ounce package crisp doughnut-
   shaped oat cereal
1 6-ounce package bite-size crisp
   rice squares
1 7-ounce package small pretzel twists
1 5¾-ounce package slim pretzel
   sticks
1 4½-ounce can pretzel bits
2 cups salad oil
2 tablespoons Worcestershire sauce
1 tablespoon garlic salt
1 tablespoon seasoned salt

Mix all ingredients in very large roaster or large pans. Bake in very slow oven (250°) 2 hours, stirring and turning mixture with wooden spoon every 15 minutes (be careful not to crush cereals). Makes 9 quarts.

Note: You can substitute equal amounts of other ready-to-eat cereals (kinds that won't crush) for any of cereal ingredients above, if you wish.

Corn-meal Thins

If you wish, freeze half recipe to use later—

½ cup milk
3 tablespoons salad oil
¼ teaspoon Worcestershire sauce
Dash bottled hot pepper sauce
½ cup sifted all-purpose flour
½ teaspoon salt
¼ teaspoon soda
1 cup yellow corn meal
Melted butter or margarine
Caraway seed—or dill,
   toasted sesame, or poppy seed

Combine first four ingredients. Sift together flour, salt, and soda, add corn meal; stir into milk mixture. Work together with fingers till dough forms a ball. Knead on lightly floured board 8 minutes.

Drop by level teaspoons onto well-greased cooky sheet, 6 to 8 at a time. Then, using rolling pin, roll out (on cooky sheet) to scant ¼-inch thick, forming about 4x3-inch oblong thins.

Bake at 350° for 6 to 7 minutes or till golden. Remove carefully from pan to rack. Brush lightly with butter and sprinkle with seeds. Makes about 4 dozen.

Corn Crackle

Peanuts add crunch to tasty snack—

1 8-ounce package corn-muffin mix
1 cup coarsely chopped salted peanuts
½ cup grated Parmesan cheese
1 teaspoon garlic salt
3 tablespoons butter, melted

Prepare corn-muffin mix according to package directions; spread evenly in well-greased 15½x10½x1-inch jellyroll pan. Sprinkle with peanuts, cheese, and garlic salt; drizzle butter over top.

Bake at 375° about 25 minutes or till crisp and lightly browned. At once cut in squares; cool slightly; remove from pan.

Parmesan Shoestrings

Empty 1 can shoestring potatoes into a shallow baking dish. Sprinkle with ½ cup grated Parmesan cheese. Heat in moderate oven (350°) till toasty.

Walnut Snack

Nuts take on a delightful herbed flavor—

Spread 1 cup California walnut halves in shallow pan. Dot with 1½ teaspoons butter or margarine. Heat in moderate oven (350°) about 15 minutes, stirring occasionally.

Remove from oven; sprinkle with 1 teaspoon onion salt. Cool on paper towels.

Scramble—it's scrumptious!

This good combination of crisp toasted cereals and nuts is perfect for game-room snacking. And the recipes makes plenty for a crowd! Nice go-with: fudge.

Snacks with a gourmet flair – delicious!

Antipasto Tray

Fresh Relish Italiano: Thinly slice tomatoes, cucumbers, and onions; separate onions in rings. Pour Italian salad dressing over (bottled or from envelope of mix). Sprinkle with salt and cracked pepper. Chill a few hours; spoon dressing over again.

Avocado Cuts with Salami: Dip slices of ripe avocado in bottled tomato French dressing. (Or use Italian salad-dressing mix, replacing water with tomato juice, according to package directions.) Alternate avocado with thin slices of salami.

Olive-stuffed Eggs: Peel 5 hard-cooked eggs; halve lengthwise. Remove yolks, mash; combine with 2 tablespoons *each* mayonnaise and chopped ripe olives, 2 teaspoons vinegar, and 1 teaspoon prepared mustard. Season to taste. Fill whites; chill. Garnish.

Marinated Artichoke Hearts: Cook a package of frozen artichoke hearts; drain. (Or drain canned artichoke hearts; halve.) Mix 2 tablespoons *each* lemon juice and olive oil, 1 clove garlic, crushed, ¼ teaspoon salt, and dash pepper; pour over artichokes. Chill; spoon marinade over a few times. At serving time, drain; dash with paprika. Tuck in thin lemon slices.

Tonno al Limone: Chill a large can of solid-pack tuna. Open can and carefully slide the wheel of tuna out onto serving dish. Squeeze juice of ½ lemon over top. Trim with lemon slice and water cress.

Chafing-dish Olives

To one 7-ounce can pitted ripe olives (undrained), add 1 to 2 cloves garlic, minced. Refrigerate several days. To serve, heat olives in small amount of olive liquid plus 2 tablespoons salad oil. Spear on picks.

Pass an Antipasto Tray!

In bowls at left: Fresh Relish Italiano and Avocado Cuts with Salami. Center: Olive-stuffed Eggs, sharp cheese. Right: Marinated Artichoke Hearts and Tonno al Limone.

Curried Olives

1 tablespoon instant minced onion
2 tablespoons lemon juice
1 tablespoon curry powder
½ cup salad oil
1½ cups drained stuffed green olives

Combine onion and lemon juice; let stand 5 minutes. Add curry powder. With electric or rotary beater, slowly beat in the salad oil. Put olives in jar; pour curry mixture over. Cover, refrigerate at least 3 days to mellow flavor. Drain before serving.

Swedish Pickled Shrimp

2 to 2½ pounds fresh or frozen
    shrimp in shells
½ cup celery tops
¼ cup mixed pickling spices
1 tablespoon salt
2 cups sliced onions
7 or 8 bay leaves
1 recipe Pickling Marinade

Cover shrimp with boiling water; add celery tops, spices, and salt. Cover and simmer for 5 minutes. Drain, then peel and devein under cold water. Alternate the cleaned shrimp, onions, and bay leaves in shallow baking dish.

Pour Pickling Marinade over shrimp. Cover; chill at least 24 hours, spooning marinade over shrimp occasionally. Remove bay leaves; serve. Pickled shrimp will keep at least a week in refrigerator. Makes 6 appetizer-size servings.

Pickling Marinade: Combine 1½ cups salad oil, ¾ cup white vinegar, 3 tablespoons capers and juice, 2½ teaspoons celery seed, 1½ teaspoons salt, and few drops bottled hot pepper sauce. Mix well.

Marinated Beef Strips

1 pound cooked sirloin steak or
    beef roast, cut in thin strips
1 small onion, thinly sliced and
    separated in rings
¾ teaspoon salt
Dash pepper
1½ tablespoons lemon juice
1 cup dairy sour cream

Combine beef, onion rings, salt, and pepper. Sprinkle with lemon juice. Stir in sour cream. Chill. Serve on lettuce. Serves 6. Famous origin: Chicago's Stock Yard Inn.

Caviar on ice—simple, smart!

Serve chilled caviar right in its container, nestled in a bed of crushed ice. This is small black caviar. Circle with lemon or lime wedges; add fluff of water cress.

Guests spread caviar on Melba toast, dash on lemon or lime juice. Then they sprinkle on their choice of finely chopped hard-cooked egg white and egg yolk, and minced onion and chives. It's the ultimate in canapes!

Broiled Stuffed Mushrooms

12 large fresh mushrooms
    • • •
½ cup drained crab meat
1 tablespoon butter
¼ cup finely chopped celery
2 tablespoons mayonnaise
1 teaspoon lemon juice
Dash salt
2 tablespoons buttered fine
    dry bread crumbs

Wash mushrooms; trim off tips of stems. Remove caps* and set aside; finely chop stems. Separate bony bits from crab meat; snip meat in fine pieces. Cook chopped mushroom stems in butter till just tender. Add crab, celery, mayonnaise, lemon juice, and salt.

Stuff mushroom caps; sprinkle with crumbs. Broil 6 inches from heat about 10 minutes. Trim with pimiento cutouts or parsley. Serve *hot*. (You'll need forks.)

*Mushrooms extra large? Pour boiling water over caps; let stand 1 minute; drain.

Jellied Consomme—trim
with sour cream, chives, lemon slices.
Calico Tomato Cooler is a
chilly soup with "bite" from zesty sauces.

Snacks to sip or spoon!

Calico Tomato Cooler

2¼ to 2½ cups tomato juice
¼ cup finely chopped celery
2 tablespoons finely chopped green
   onions and tops
2 teaspoons soy sauce
1 teaspoon Worcestershire sauce
Few drops bottled hot pepper sauce

Combine ingredients. Salt to taste. Chill thoroughly. Float a few unpared cucumber slices. (To flute edges, run tines of fork down cucumber; slice.) Makes 5 servings.

Jellied Consomme

Chill canned condensed consomme in refrigerator at least 3 hours (or 1 hour in freezer). Spoon into chilled sherbets or glass bowl. Garnish with lemon slices and sour cream. Sprinkle with chives.

Sparkling Borsch

Color is a lovely red, flavor's delightful!—

⅔ cup finely chopped cooked or
   canned beets
Beet liquid plus water to make 1 cup
2 cans condensed consomme
2 tablespoons lemon juice

• • •

Sour cream
Chopped parsley

Combine beets, beet liquid, and consomme. Heat and stir just till blended.

Add lemon juice and chill thoroughly. (Soup will look jellied.) Stir before ladling into chilled cups or bowls. Top with generous dollops of sour cream; sprinkle with chopped parsley. Makes 6 servings.

Serve with dainty sandwiches and iced tea for a cool snack. Or serve as appetizer.

Gourmet Chicken Soup

1 can condensed cream of
   chicken soup
1¾ cups chicken broth
¼ teaspoon tarragon

. . .

½ cup whipping cream, whipped
Paprika

Combine first three ingredients in blender
or shaker. Blend or shake till smooth, about
10 seconds. Heat thoroughly.

   Serve piping hot. Top each serving with
a fluff of whipped cream; sprinkle with a
dash of paprika. Pass assorted crackers.
Makes 5 or 6 servings.

Tomato Soupshake

*Creamy-smooth with a nice tomato-y taste. Add
an egg for extra protein, turn shake into a
soupnog—it's a quick summer lunch!—*

1 can condensed tomato soup
1 cup half-and-half or light cream
½ teaspoon nutmeg
¼ teaspoon salt
1 egg (optional)

Combine all ingredients in blender or
shaker. Blend or shake till mixture is
smooth. Chill. (For thinner soupshake, add
a little milk.)

   Serve in chilled cups or glasses. Sprinkle
with nutmeg. Makes 4 or 5 servings.

Cucumber Soup

1 to 1½ cups grated or ground
   pared cucumber*
1 quart buttermilk
1 tablespoon chopped green onions
1 teaspoon salt
¼ cup finely chopped parsley
½ teaspoon monosodium glutamate
Dash pepper

Combine ingredients. Mix well Cover and
chill thoroughly (about 4 hours). Mix
again, just before serving in chilled cups.
Garnish with slices of cucumber and parsley sprigs. Makes 8 to 10 servings.

   *Scoop out and discard seeds before
grating or putting through food chopper.
One medium cucumber will give about ⅔
cup grated or ground cucumber.

Tomato Soupshake—quick!

Chilly, yet filling—with bread sticks or
crackers, it's a perfect midday snack. Keep
on tap in the refrigerator for any time!

Cucumber Soup—tangy, cold

The good tartness of buttermilk is blended
with crunchy bits of cucumber. For garnish,
set fluted slices of cucumber afloat. Serve in
an ice bucket to hold in the chill.

Tomato Mist

1 46-ounce can or 2 No. 2 cans
  (5 to 6 cups) tomato juice
¼ cup lemon juice
1 teaspoon sugar
¼ teaspoon onion powder
2 teaspoons Worcestershire sauce
2 teaspoons prepared horseradish
Salt to taste

Combine all ingredients. Chill thoroughly. Stir well before serving. Garnish with lemon slices. Makes 9 to 12 servings.

Tomato Toddy

1 can condensed tomato soup
1 can condensed beef broth
1 soup can water
¼ teaspoon marjoram
¼ teaspoon thyme
Oyster crackers

Combine ingredients. Bring to boiling; reduce heat and simmer gently 2 minutes. Dot with butter. Float 1 or 2 oyster crackers in each cupful. Makes 4 or 5 servings.

Easy Vegetable Refresher

Heat canned vegetable-juice cocktail, stir in butter—1 teaspoon for each cup. Serve in mugs. That's all there is to it!

Cranberry Delight

Pretty garnish: Float halved orange slices—

2 tablespoons whole cloves
1 tablespoon whole allspice
12 inches stick cinnamon, broken

• • •

½ to ⅔ cup sugar
¼ teaspoon salt
5 cups water
2½ cups grapefruit juice
2 1-pound cans (4 cups) jellied
  cranberry sauce, mashed

Tie spices in small piece of cheesecloth. Add to other ingredients and bring slowly to boiling. Cover and simmer 5 minutes; remove spices. Add a few drops of red food coloring, if desired. Serve in mugs. Makes about 20 half-cup servings.

Lime Frost

These are the tall beauties on the cover!—

1 6-ounce can frozen limeade
  concentrate
5 to 6 cups finely crushed ice
Green food coloring

Empty frozen concentrate into chilled blender. Add ice, 1 cup at a time, blending well after each addition. Stop blender several times and push ice down with rubber scraper. Add few drops green food coloring, if desired. Serve pronto in 6 tall glasses with straws and spoons. Serves 6.

Banana Nog

1 medium fully ripe banana
½ pint (1 cup) vanilla ice cream
1 6-ounce can (⅔ cup) chilled
  evaporated milk
1 egg
1 teaspoon vanilla

Combine all ingredients in electric blender or drink mixer. Whiz about 30 seconds or till blended. Pour into chilled glasses; sprinkle with nutmeg. Makes 2 servings.

Cocoa

5 to 6 tablespoons cocoa
  (regular type, dry)
4 to 6 tablespoons sugar
Dash salt
½ cup water
3½ cups milk

Mix together cocoa, sugar, and salt; add water. Cook and stir 3 minutes. Slowly stir in milk; heat to boiling point (do not boil). Beat with rotary beater just before serving. Makes 6 servings.

Hot Chocolate, French Style

Heat 2½ 1-ounce squares unsweetened chocolate and ½ cup water over low heat; stir till chocolate melts. Add ⅔ cup sugar and ½ teaspoon salt. Bring to boiling, reduce heat; simmer 4 minutes. Cool to room temperature. Fold in ½ cup whipping cream, whipped. Store in refrigerator.

To serve, place 1 heaping tablespoon in each cup and fill with hot milk; stir well. Makes 8 to 10 teacup servings.

Treats for a sweet tooth

Remarkable Fudge

4 cups sugar
1 14½-ounce can (1⅔ cups)
    evaporated milk
1 cup butter or margarine

. . .

1 12-ounce package (2 cups) semisweet
    chocolate pieces
1 pint marshmallow creme
1 teaspoon vanilla
1 cup broken California walnuts

Butter sides of heavy 3-quart saucepan. In it combine sugar, milk, and butter. Cook over medium heat to soft-ball stage (236°), stirring frequently.

Remove from heat; add chocolate, marshmallow creme, vanilla, and nuts. Beat till chocolate is melted and blended.

Pour into buttered 9x9x2-inch pan.* Score in squares while warm, and if desired, top with walnut halves; cut when firm. Makes 3 dozen 1½-inch pieces.

*Or use a 13x9x2-inch pan.

Pop Snacks

Chewy-crisp clusters of popcorn and nuts—

2½ quarts popped corn
1 pound (2¼ cups) light brown sugar
½ cup light corn syrup
½ cup water
½ cup butter or margarine
2 teaspoons salt
1 tablespoon vanilla
1 cup salted peanuts

Keep popped corn hot and crisp in slow oven (300° to 325°). In large saucepan, combine sugar, syrup, water, butter, and salt. Cook over moderate heat, stirring occasionally, until syrup reaches hard-crack (290°). Remove from heat; stir in vanilla.

In large buttered bowl or pan, mix nuts and popcorn. Pour syrup in fine stream over mixture. Working quickly, mix well until kernels are completely coated.

Spread out thin on buttered cooky sheets. Quickly separate into bite-size clusters with 2 buttered forks. Cool. Makes 3½ quarts.

Peanut-butter Crisps

Caramel-y, delicious, and quick as a wink!—

Mix 3 cups crisp rice cereal and 1 cup salted peanuts; set aside.

Combine ½ cup sugar and ½ cup light corn syrup. Cook, stirring constantly, till mixture comes to a full rolling boil. Remove from heat. Stir in ½ cup peanut butter and ½ teaspoon vanilla.

Immediately pour hot syrup over cereal mixture, stirring gently to coat. Pat cereal evenly into buttered 8x8x2-inch pan. Cool and cut in 2-inch bars. (Makes 16.)

Tutti-frutti Bars

¼ cup butter or margarine
½ pound marshmallows
½ teaspoon vanilla
½ cup chopped candied cherries
½ cup coarsely chopped pecans

. . .

1 5½-ounce package crisp rice cereal

Heat butter and marshmallows in double boiler till thick and syrupy. Beat in vanilla. Add cherries and pecans.

Place cereal in large bowl. Pour marshmallow mixture over, stirring briskly. Press into a greased 9x9x2-inch pan. Press extra cherries and nuts into top of mixture, if desired. Let stand till firm enough to cut, about 1 hour. Makes 24 bars.

Peanut Clusters

1 8-ounce package semisweet chocolate,
    or 1⅓ cups semisweet
    chocolate pieces
½ pound roasted Spanish peanuts

Melt chocolate in top of double boiler, over *hot, not boiling* water; remove from heat. Stir in peanuts. Drop from teaspoon onto waxed paper-lined cooky sheet. Chill in refrigerator several hours. Store in *cool* place. Makes 2½ dozen clusters.

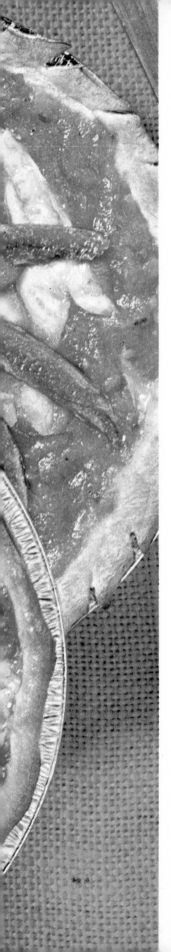

Pickups for after 10 p.m.

Pizza—Italian-style crusts with a variety of spirited fillings!

Sandwiches—high and hearty— Perfect for easygoing entertaining!

Treats for "doughnut 'n cider time" plus coffeecake, waffles, pancakes that are just right with coffee!

← *From our pinwheel, take your pick of pizza!*
Clockwise from upper left: Pepperoni Ring with a hot-roll-mix crust; pizza from a package—we added Mozzarella cheese and anchovy fillets; Sausage Pizza—a start-from-scratch favorite; Cheese Pizza, crust from biscuit mix and yeast.

Pizza makes a party!

Pizza has become as American as apple pie! And no wonder—it fits right into our scheme of simple-to-do snacks. These are so good—plan on seconds!

Sausage Pizza

For real Italian flavor, you can't beat it!—

1 pound Italian sausage

· · ·

1 1-pound can (2 cups) tomatoes
1 recipe Pizza Crust
Salt
Coarse-cracked pepper
8 ounces Mozzarella cheese, *thin sliced* and torn in pieces
Olive oil (about ¼ cup)

· · ·

1 6-ounce can (⅔ cup) tomato paste
2 cloves garlic, minced
1 tablespoon crushed oregano
1 tablespoon basil leaves
¼ cup grated Parmesan or Romano cheese

Break sausage in small bits in skillet; fry slowly until lightly browned, about 10 minutes, stirring occasionally; drain off fat.

Drain tomatoes, reserving ½ cup tomato juice. Cut up tomatoes and place in layers on prepared Pizza Crust circles. Sprinkle with salt and pepper, then cover with the Mozzarella cheese. Drizzle with some of the olive oil (about 1 tablespoon on each pizza). Sprinkle with sausage.

Combine tomato paste, reserved tomato juice, garlic, and herbs, mixing well; spread over sausage. Dash generously with salt and pepper. Scatter Parmesan cheese over all. Drizzle with more olive oil (about 1 tablespoon on each).

Bake in hot oven (425°) about 18 minutes or till crust is done. Makes 2 pizzas.

Pizza Crust

1 package active dry yeast
1 cup *warm* water
3½ cups sifted all-purpose flour
1 tablespoon olive oil
1 teaspoon salt

· · ·

2 tablespoons olive oil

Soften active dry yeast in the warm water. Beat in 1½ *cups of the flour;* mix in 1 tablespoon olive oil and the salt. Stir in remaining flour. Knead on lightly floured surface until smooth and elastic, about 12 minutes. (Dough will be very firm.)

Place in lightly greased mixing bowl, turn to bring greased side up. Cover and let rise in a warm place until more than double, about 1½ hours. (Dough will have a yeasty odor.) Punch down, cover, and place in refrigerator until cold.

Cut dough in 2 parts. On lightly floured surface, roll each in a 12-inch circle about ⅛ inch thick. Place on greased cooky sheets or 12-inch pizza pans, turning edge of dough up slightly. Gash bottom about every 2 inches to prevent bubbles. Brush each crust with 1 tablespoon olive oil. Fill and bake—see Sausage Pizza recipe. Makes 2 12-inch crusts.

Pizzaburgers

1 pound ground beef
½ cup chopped onion
1 6-ounce can (⅔ cup) tomato paste
1 teaspoon salt
1 teaspoon crushed oregano
¼ teaspoon garlic powder

· · ·

6 buns, split, toasted, buttered

In skillet, brown beef and cook onion till tender but not brown. Add tomato paste and seasonings. Simmer uncovered about 15 minutes. Spoon hot meat mixture between or over bun halves. If you like, slip onion rings and/or thinly sliced Mozzarella cheese into each bun. Makes 6 servings.

Pepperoni Pizza

Hot-roll mix makes a Naples-style crust—

1 package hot-roll mix
Olive oil
¾ pound small pepperoni, thinly
   sliced
½ cup shredded Parmesan or
   Romano cheese
2 8-ounce cans (2 cups) seasoned
   tomato sauce
1 tablespoon crushed oregano
1 teaspoon anise seed
4 cloves garlic, crushed
1 6-ounce package Mozzarella cheese,
   thinly sliced, cut in triangles

Prepare dough from hot roll mix, following package directions, but *using 1 cup warm water* and *omitting egg. Do not let rise.* Divide dough in half. On greased baking sheets, pat or roll each piece of dough into a 12-inch circle*. Clip edges at 1-inch intervals and press so they'll stand up slightly. Brush dough with olive oil.

Reserve enough pepperoni slices for trim (about 20); scatter remainder over dough and sprinkle with *half* the Parmesan cheese. Combine tomato sauce, oregano, anise seed, and garlic, mixing well; spread over pepperoni. Top with a big circle of overlapping Mozzarella-cheese triangles; sprinkle with remaining Parmesan. Trim with a ring of reserved pepperoni slices. Bake in very hot oven (450°) about 20 minutes or till crust is done. Makes 2 pizzas.

*Or use two greased 12-inch pizza pans; omit clipping edges of dough.

Salami Pizza Sandwiches

⅔ cup canned pizza sauce
8 slices bread
4 large or 8 small slices salami
4 slices sharp process American cheese
Garlic salt or salt
Soft butter or margarine

Spread pizza sauce on one side of each bread slice. Top 4 with salami slices, then with cheese; sprinkle with garlic salt. Add remaining bread slices, sauce side down.

Generously butter top and bottom of sandwiches. Grill both sides on griddle, grill, or in a skillet until sandwiches are toasted and cheese melts. Makes 4.

Cheese Pizza

Canned pizza sauce and a crust of biscuit mix plus yeast speed this no-meat pizza—

1 package active dry yeast
¾ cup *warm* water
2½ cups packaged biscuit mix
3 5½-ounce cans (2¼ cups)
   pizza sauce
1 chopped onion
½ cup chopped green pepper
1 6-ounce can (1⅓ cups) broiled
   sliced mushrooms, drained
1 pound Mozzarella cheese,
   thinly sliced
Olive oil
Coarse-ground pepper and
   crushed oregano
Yellow and red pickled banana peppers

Soften yeast in warm water. Add biscuit mix; beat vigorously 2 minutes. On surface dusted with biscuit mix, knead till smooth, 25 strokes. Divide dough in 4ths. On greased baking sheets, roll each piece paper-thin to a 10-inch circle or pat into four 9-inch pizza pans; turn up edges of dough, and crimp, if desired. Brush dough with olive oil.

Cut 16 triangles of Mozzarella cheese and set aside for trim; tear remaining cheese in pieces and place over crust.

Scatter onion, green pepper, and mushrooms over cheese, dash with salt. Drizzle with pizza sauce and dash generously with coarse pepper and oregano. Top with the reserved cheese triangles. Cut triangles of pickled peppers and arrange atop the cheese. Bake in hot oven (425°) about 15 minutes or till crust is done. Makes 4.

Inside-out Pizza

Spread inner surfaces of sandwich with spaghetti or pizza sauce; sprinkle one of them with basil. Add several slices of Provolone cheese to make a generous filling. Brush the outer surfaces of the sandwich with soft butter. Grill slowly on ungreased griddle, sandwich grill, or in skillet.

Piquant options: Sprinkle 2 or 3 drops of bottled hot pepper sauce inside each sandwich. Or shake grated Parmesan or Romano cheese on one inner surface.

Sandwich specials

Grilled Corned Beef 'n Rye

For real elegance, make filling of up to 12 paper-thin slices of corned beef—

> 12 slices pumpernickel
> ½ cup Thousand Island dressing
> 6 slices Swiss cheese
> 6 tablespoons drained sauerkraut
> ¼ to ½ pound cooked or canned
>   corned beef, sliced very thin

Spread 6 slices of bread with Thousand Island dressing. Top each with cheese, 1 tablespoon sauerkraut, sliced corned beef, and second slice of bread.

Butter top and bottom of sandwiches. Grill on both sides till hot and cheese is melty. Makes 6.

Chef's Salad Special

Brown big brown-and-serve French rolls (about 8 inches long) according to package directions. Split rolls in half, but *not quite through*. (If you like, scoop out some of the centers to make room for filling.)

For each supersize sandwich, line bottom half of roll with romaine lettuce; drizzle with 1 teaspoon French dressing. Pile on slices of chicken; dash with salt and pepper. Add 1 or 2 slices of boiled ham and Swiss cheese, halved to fit roll.

Top with hard-cooked egg slices; salt. Cover with romaine and tomato slices; season. Drizzle with 2 teaspoons more dressing. Add roll tops; anchor with picks.

Grilled Cheese Italiano

For each sandwich, top slice of Italian bread with a slice of Mozzarella and a slice or two of salami. Dash on oregano and top with second bread slice.

Generously butter top and bottom of sandwich. Grill on both sides till sandwich is toasty and golden brown. Anchor with cherry pepper speared on toothpick, as shown on frontispiece. Pass olives, relishes.

Dilly Hamburgers

No ordinary burgers, these. Dill-flavored sour cream topper puts them in a class by themselves!—

> 1 to 1½ pounds ground beef
> Salt and pepper
> 1 cup dairy sour cream
> 1 teaspoon prepared mustard
> 1 tablespoon dill seed or 3
>   tablespoons snipped fresh dill
> • • •
> 4 to 6 hamburger buns, split, buttered
>   and grilled

Lightly pat meat into 4 to 6 patties, about ¼ to ½ inch thick. Grill on lightly greased griddle or in skillet till done to your liking, turning once; season with salt and pepper.

Combine sour cream, mustard, and dill seed; spoon atop burgers. For fun, top each with fresh dill sprig, or olive slices. Serve on grilled buttered buns, with "lids" tipped back. Serve with olives, potato chips, ice-cold fruit punch.

Broiled Turkey Sandwich

> 2 cups chopped cooked turkey
> ½ cup chopped celery
> ⅓ cup mayonnaise or salad dressing
> ¼ cup chopped green pepper
> 1 tablespoon chopped onion
> 2 teaspoons lemon juice
> Salt and pepper
> • • •
> 6 slices bread
> Soft butter or margarine
> • • •
> 1 cup shredded sharp process
>   American cheese

Combine first 6 ingredients; add salt and pepper to taste. Toast bread on one side; butter untoasted side.

Spread turkey mixture on buttered side of bread, covering all edges. Broil 4 inches from heat about 3 minutes or till turkey mixture is heated through. Sprinkle with cheese; broil about 1 minute or till cheese is bubbly. Makes 6 servings.

Grilled Turkey Hamwich—just the thing for unexpected guests

On one slice of bread, stack thin slices of roast turkey, canned jellied cranberry sauce, and boiled ham. Top with second slice of bread. Generously butter top and bottom of sandwiches with soft butter or margarine.

Grill both sides of sandwiches on griddle, sandwich grill, or in a skillet till bread is toasted a golden brown.

A nice go-with: Canned pineapple slices and spicy crab apples; grill last few minutes.

Quick Turkey Sandwich Fillings: Combine two parts *each* chopped cooked turkey and broken California walnuts, with 1 part drained crushed pineapple. Moisten with mayonnaise. Spread on buttered bread slices.

Or mix chopped cooked turkey with finely chopped celery, chopped sweet pickle; add salad dressing or mayonnaise to moisten.

Meat-Cheese Open Facers

Combine 1 cup shredded sharp process cheese, 3 tablespoons mayonnaise, and 2 tablespoons chopped green onion.

Slice one 12-ounce can luncheon meat in 12 thin slices. Lightly spread 6 slices toasted bread with prepared mustard; top each with 2 slices of luncheon meat. Spread meat with cheese mixture. Broil 4 inches from heat about 3 minutes or till cheese melts. Makes 6 open-face sandwiches.

Hot Ham Buns

Poppy seeds add a touch of old-world flavor. Try rye hamburger buns for a change—

¼ cup soft butter or margarine
2 tablespoons prepared horseradish-mustard
2 teaspoons poppy seed
2 tablespoons finely chopped onion
• • •
4 hamburger buns, split
4 thin slices boiled ham
4 slices Swiss process cheese

Mix butter, mustard, poppy seed and onion; spread on cut surfaces of buns.

Tuck a slice of ham and cheese in each bun. Arrange on baking sheet. Bake in moderate oven (350°) about 20 minutes or till hot through. Makes 4 sandwiches.

Deviled-ham Rollwiches

4 brown-and-serve hard rolls
Soft butter or margarine
Prepared mustard
1 4½-ounce can deviled ham
• • •
8 thin slices peeled tomato, halved
1 medium green pepper, cut in strips
1 small onion, sliced thin and in rings
• • •
8 narrow strips American cheese

Halve rolls lengthwise. Broil, cut sides down, till nicely browned. Spread cut sides with soft butter, mustard, and ham. Top each half with 2 pieces of tomato, green-pepper strips, and onion rings.

Broil 3 to 4 inches from heat 4 to 5 minutes. Place cheese strips atop; broil just till cheese melts. Makes 4 servings.

Broiler Tuna Burgers

Combine one 6½- or 7-ounce can tuna, flaked, with 2 tablespoons chopped onion and 2 tablespoons chopped sweet pickles. Moisten with ¼ cup mayonnaise.

Split and toast 5 hamburger buns; butter bottom halves and spread with tuna mixture. Top each with slice of sharp process cheese. Broil 5 inches from heat 4 minutes or till cheese melts. Add bun toppers. Makes 5 sandwiches.

Cider-time doughnuts

Coconut Cake Doughnuts

Plump, tender, with "special-occasion" flavor—

2 eggs
½ cup sugar

• • •

¼ cup milk
2 tablespoons melted shortening
or salad oil
2⅓ cups sifted all-purpose flour
2 teaspoons baking powder
½ teaspoon salt
½ cup flaked coconut

Beat eggs with sugar till light; add milk and cooled shortening. Add sifted dry ingredients and coconut; stir just till blended. Chill several hours.

Roll on lightly floured surface to ½ inch thick. Cut out doughnuts with doughnut cutter. Fry in deep hot fat (375°) till brown; turn and brown other side (about 1 minute per side). Drain on paper towel. Sprinkle with sugar. Makes 1 dozen.

Fruited Doughnut Balls

Fruit-filled and sugar-coated—

2 cups sifted all-purpose flour
½ teaspoon soda
¼ teaspoon salt

• • •

2 beaten egg yolks
½ cup sugar
½ cup sour milk
2 tablespoons orange juice

• • •

½ cup finely chopped pecans
¼ cup chopped raisins
¼ cup finely chopped dates
1 teaspoon grated orange peel

Sift together flour, soda, and salt. Combine egg yolks, sugar, sour milk, and orange juice; stir into dry ingredients. Add nuts, fruits, and peel. Stir to blend.

Drop by teaspoons into deep hot fat (350°) and fry 4 to 5 minutes or till brown on all sides, turning once. Drain on paper towel. Roll in sugar. Makes 2 dozen.

Filled Doughnuts

Inside these puffy half-moons—a fruit surprise—

2 packages active dry yeast or
2 cakes compressed yeast
½ cup water
¾ cup milk, scalded
⅓ cup shortening
¼ cup sugar
1 teaspoon salt
2 eggs
4½ to 5 cups sifted all-purpose flour

• • •

18 prunes
¼ cup sugar

Soften the active dry yeast in *warm* water, compressed yeast in *lukewarm* water. Combine milk, shortening, ¼ cup sugar, and salt; stir till shortening is dissolved. Cool to lukewarm. Add yeast, eggs, and 2 cups flour; beat well. Add enough remaining flour to make soft dough. Turn out on lightly floured surface and knead till smooth and elastic, about 8 to 10 minutes. Place in a greased bowl, turning to grease surface. Cover; let rise till double, about 50 minutes.

Meanwhile, cook prunes according to package directions, adding ¼ cup sugar at beginning of cooking. Cool; halve, pit.

Cut dough in half for easy handling. Roll ⅜ inch thick; cut with a 2½-inch round cutter. Place a prune half in each round of dough; fold dough over prune and seal edges; cover and let rise till almost double, about 20 minutes.

Fry in deep hot fat (375°) till golden, about 1 minute on each side. Drain on paper towel. Roll in sugar or shake lightly in paper sack. Serve warm. Makes 3 dozen.

Take your choice of doughnuts →

We show New Orleans Square Doughnuts, Fluffy Potato Doughnuts, Coconut Cake Doughnuts, Fruited Doughnut Balls, Filled Doughnuts, and Crullers. Go-with: hot cider with orange slice and cinnamon-stick stirrer.

Crullers

2 packages active dry yeast
½ cup warm water
½ cup milk, scalded
⅓ cup sugar
1½ teaspoons salt
¼ cup shortening
3¼ to 3¾ cups sifted
　　all-purpose flour
1 slightly beaten egg

Soften yeast in warm water. Mix milk, sugar, salt, shortening; stir till shortening melts; cool to lukewarm. Add 1 cup of flour; beat well; add egg and softened yeast. Add enough of remaining flour to make moderately soft dough.

Knead on lightly floured surface about 8 minutes. Place in greased bowl, turning once to grease the surface; cover, let rise till doubled, 1 to 1½ hours. Punch down, let rise again till double. Punch down and let rest 10 minutes.

On lightly floured surface roll into 12x9-inch rectangle, ½ inch thick. Cut in half crosswise; cut each half into 12 strips. Roll each strip under hands to make 10-inch strip; twist for crullers. Cover, let rise about 45 minutes or till almost doubled in size.

Fry in deep hot fat (375°) about 2 minutes, turning once; drain. Brush with confectioners' icing to glaze. Makes 2 dozen.

Fluffy Potato Doughnuts

3 eggs
1⅓ cups sugar
½ teaspoon vanilla
1 cup mashed potatoes, cooled*
2 tablespoons melted shortening
　　or salad oil
4 cups sifted all-purpose flour
6 teaspoons baking powder
2 teaspoons nutmeg
1 teaspoon salt
½ cup milk

Beat eggs with sugar and vanilla till light. Add potatoes and shortening. Sift together dry ingredients; add alternately with milk to potato mixture, beating well. Chill dough 3 hours.

Roll out half of dough at a time, keeping other half chilled. Roll on floured surface to ⅜ inch thick. Cut with floured 1½-inch doughnut cutter; chill 15 minutes.

Fry in deep, hot fat (375°) about 3 minutes or till brown, turning once; drain. Dip in sugar. Makes 2 to 2½ dozen.

*Cook 2 medium potatoes; mash with butter and milk to make light and fluffy.

New Orleans Square Doughnuts

1 cake compressed yeast
¼ cup lukewarm water
¾ cup milk, scalded
¼ cup shortening
¼ cup sugar
1 teaspoon salt
1 egg
About 3½ cups sifted all-purpose flour

Soften yeast in lukewarm water. Combine milk, shortening, sugar and salt; cool to lukewarm. Add 1 cup of the flour; beat well. Add softened yeast and egg; mix. Add enough of remaining flour to make soft dough. Turn out on lightly floured surface; knead till smooth (about 8 minutes). Place in greased bowl, turn once to grease surface. Cover; let rise till double (about 1¼ hours). Punch down. Let rise again till double (about 55 minutes).

Roll out dough to 14x10-inch rectangle ⅓ inch thick. Cut in 2-inch squares. Let rise till light (30 to 40 minutes). Fry in deep hot fat (375°) about 4 minutes or till browned, turning once. Drain. While warm, dip in sugar. Makes 3 dozen.

Midnight-coffee treats

Ginger Muffins

½ cup shortening
½ cup sugar
1 egg
1 cup molasses
3 cups sifted all-purpose flour
1½ teaspoons soda
½ teaspoon salt
1 teaspoon cinnamon
1 teaspoon ginger
½ teaspoon cloves
1 cup hot water

Cream together shortening and sugar. Beat in egg, then molasses. Sift together dry ingredients; stir into molasses mixture. Gradually add hot water, beating till mixture is smooth.

Fill greased muffin pans ⅔ full. Bake at 375° for 20 to 25 minutes. Makes 2 dozen muffins. Serve warm.

Spicy Raisin Coffeecake

½ cup butter or margarine
1 cup sugar
2 eggs
1 teaspoon vanilla
1 cup dairy sour cream
2 cups sifted all-purpose flour
1½ teaspoons baking powder
1 teaspoon soda
¼ teaspoon salt

• • •

1 cup broken walnuts
½ cup sugar
1 teaspoon cinnamon
1½ cups seedless raisins

Cream together butter and 1 cup sugar till fluffy. Add eggs and vanilla; beat well. Blend in sour cream. Sift together next 4 ingredients; stir into creamed mixture; mix well. Spread *half* the batter in greased 9x9x2-inch pan. Mix nuts, ½ cup sugar, and cinnamon; sprinkle *half* over batter. Sprinkle raisins over. Spoon on remaining batter. Top with remaining nut mixture. Bake in moderate oven (350°) about 40 minutes. Cut in squares. Serve warm.

Golden Apricot Roll-ups

1 cup packaged pancake mix
½ cup apricot jam
2 slightly beaten eggs
½ cup corn-flake crumbs
2 tablespoons butter or margarine

Prepare pancake mix according to package directions, but using *1 cup milk, 1 egg,* and *1 tablespoon salad oil or melted shortening.* Bake on griddle, as directed on package. Spread about a tablespoon apricot jam over each hot cake. Roll up. Dip rolls in egg, then in corn-flake crumbs. Place, seam side down, in skillet. Brown in butter over low heat. Serve hot. Makes 8 roll-ups.

Peanut-butter Waffles

1 cup packaged pancake mix
2 tablespoons sugar
⅓ cup chunk-style peanut butter
1 egg
1 cup milk
2 tablespoons salad oil

Combine all ingredients. Beat with rotary or electric beater till almost smooth. (There will be a few lumps.) Bake in preheated waffle baker. Makes eight 4-inch waffles. Pass butter, jelly, or syrup.

Deviled Ham Roll-ups

Bake 8 thin pancakes from packaged mix. Stir one 4½-ounce can deviled ham to fluff up; spread about a tablespoon of ham over each hot cake. Roll; keep warm. Serve with Whipped Maple Butter and Cranbutter Sauce.

Whipped Maple Butter: Cream ½ butter till light and fluffy; gradually beat in ½ cup maple syrup or maple-flavored syrup. Turn into bowl and swirl top. Makes 1 cup.

Cranbutter Sauce: Heat one 1-pound can whole cranberry sauce with ¼ cup *each* brown sugar and butter till sugar dissolves, stirring occasionally. Remove from heat; add ½ teaspoon vanilla; serve warm.

When it's your turn to serve the club...

Bring on a spectacular dessert that tastes wonderful, and your party is an almost-certain success! Turn the page for desserts to make any club meeting a memorable event! Hostesses will be happy, too—the work is all done ahead!

← *Flapper Pudding, in the superlative class*

Hailed as the cat's pajamas around 1928, Flapper Pudding is a treasure still. "So simple even a flapper could make it," this day-before dessert makes hostessing a snap. What's more, it's luscious—butter-and-egg rich, fruit fresh, nut crisp!

Fabulous desserts for happy hostessing!

Flapper Pudding

1 cup fine vanilla-wafer crumbs
¾ cup soft butter or margarine
2 cups sifted confectioners' sugar
2 egg yolks*
2 stiff-beaten egg whites*

. . .

1 9-ounce can crushed pineapple,
well drained
½ cup chopped California walnuts

Spread *half* of vanilla-wafer crumbs on bottom of 10x6x1½-inch baking dish. Cream butter; gradually add confectioners' sugar, beating till light and fluffy. Add egg yolks, one at a time, beating well after each addition. Beat 1 minute more. Fold in egg whites (mixture may look curdled); beat at medium speed for a few *seconds* or till smooth. Fold in pineapple and nuts. Carefully spread mixture over crumbs. Top with remaining crumbs.

Chill till firm, 5 hours or overnight. Cut in 10 squares. Garnish with cherries.

*Have eggs at room temperature.

Date Bridge Dessert

Crush 12 chocolate sandwich cookies (about 1⅓ cups crumbs); reserve ¼ cup crumbs. Spread remaining crumbs in bottom of 10x6x1½-inch baking dish.

In saucepan, combine 1 cup pitted dates, cut up, ¾ cup water and ¼ teaspoon salt. Bring to a boil, then simmer about 3 minutes. Remove from heat; add ¼ pound (16) marshmallows or 2 cups tiny marshmallows; stir till marshmallows melt. Cool to room temperature, about 20 minutes.

Stir in ½ cup chopped California walnuts. Spread over crumbs in dish. Whip 1 cup whipping cream with ½ teaspoon vanilla; swirl over date mixture. Sprinkle with reserved crumbs. Chill overnight. Cut in squares to serve. Makes 8 servings.

Chocolate-Pecan Squares

2 4-ounce packages sweet cooking
chocolate
1 tablespoon water
4 beaten egg yolks
2 tablespoons sifted confectioners'
sugar
½ cup chopped pecans
4 stiff-beaten egg whites
1 6-ounce can (⅔ cup) evaporated
milk, chilled *icy cold* and whipped
Vanilla wafers

In double boiler, melt chocolate with water. Remove from heat; stir in egg yolks, then sugar. Cool to room temperature, then stir in pecans. Fold in egg whites and whipped evaporated milk. Cover bottom and sides of 8x8x2-inch baking dish with vanilla wafers. Top with *half* of the chocolate mixture, then with a layer of wafers.

Carefully spoon on remaining chocolate. Trim with wafer halves. Chill several hours or overnight. Cut in 9 squares.

Chocolate Chiffon Dessert

1 envelope (1 tablespoon) unflavored
gelatin
¼ cup cold water
⅔ cup chocolate-flavored syrup
½ teaspoon vanilla
1 cup evaporated milk, chilled *icy cold*
Wafer Crust

Soften gelatin in cold water. Heat syrup; add gelatin and stir till gelatin dissolves. Cool to room temperature. Add vanilla.

In chilled bowl, whip milk; fold in chocolate mixture. Chill till mixture mounds *slightly* when spooned. Pour over Wafer Crust. Chill firm. Cut in 9 squares.

Wafer Crust: Mix 1 cup vanilla-wafer crumbs, ¼ cup chopped walnuts, 3 tablespoons melted butter; press firmly in bottom of 8x8x2-inch pan. Chill.

Swiss Pudding Mold

    ¾ cup sugar
    1 envelope (1 tablespoon)
      unflavored gelatin
    Dash salt
    1¼ cups cold water
    2 egg whites
    ¼ teaspoon shredded lemon peel
    2 tablespoons lemon juice
    1 cup dairy sour cream
    1 cup whipping cream

Thoroughly mix sugar, gelatin, salt, and cold water. Place over medium heat, stirring constantly, till gelatin dissolves. Chill till partially set. Add egg whites, lemon peel, and lemon juice; beat till fluffy. Chill till mixture is partially set.

Fold sour cream into gelatin mixture. Whip cream and fold in. Pile into a 6-cup mold or 9 or 10 individual molds. Chill till firm, 6 hours or overnight. Unmold. Serve with sweetened fresh berries, peaches, or other fruit. Makes 9 or 10 servings.

Strawberry Swirl

    2 cups sliced fresh strawberries*
    2 tablespoons sugar
    1 3-ounce package strawberry-
      flavored gelatin
    1 cup boiling water
    ½ pound marshmallows
    ½ cup milk
    1 cup whipping cream, whipped
    Crumb Crust

Sprinkle sugar over fresh berries; let stand ½ hour. Dissolve gelatin in boiling water. Drain strawberries,* reserving juice. Add water to juice to make 1 cup; add to gelatin. Chill till partially set.

Meanwhile, combine marshmallows and milk; heat and stir till marshmallows melt. Cool thoroughly; fold in whipped cream.

Add berries to gelatin, then swirl in marshmallow mixture to marble. Pour into Crumb Crust. Chill till set. Cut into squares. Makes 9 or 12 servings.

Crumb Crust: Mix 1 cup graham-cracker crumbs, 1 tablespoon sugar, and ¼ cup butter, melted. Press firmly into bottom of a 9x9x2-inch baking dish. Chill.

*Or use one 10-ounce package frozen sliced strawberries, thawed.

Pudding 'n Pineapple Cake

    1½ cups cream-style cottage cheese
    Milk
    1 package lemon pudding-and-pie
      filling
    1 envelope unflavored gelatin
    1 9-ounce can crushed pineapple
    2 egg whites
    ¼ cup sugar
    Graham Crust

Drain cottage cheese, reserving liquid; add milk to liquid to measure 2¼ cups. Beat the drained cheese till fluffy.

In saucepan, mix pudding-and-pie filling and gelatin; prepare according to *label directions for pie filling*, using the 2¼ cups milk instead of water. Stir in pineapple (with syrup) and cottage cheese.

Beat egg whites till soft peaks form. Gradually add sugar, beating to stiff peaks; fold into gelatin mixture. Pour into Graham Crust. Chill till set. Cut in 10 or 12 squares; trim with berries.

Graham Crust: Mix 1¼ cups fine graham-cracker crumbs, 2 tablespoons sugar, ⅓ cup melted butter; press onto bottom and sides of 11½x7½x1½-inch baking dish.

Molded Ambrosia

    1 cup graham-cracker crumbs
    ¼ cup butter or margarine, melted
    1 9-ounce can (1 cup)
      crushed pineapple
    1 3-ounce package orange-flavored
      gelatin
    ⅓ cup sugar
    1 cup hot water
    1 cup dairy sour cream
    ¼ teaspoon vanilla
    1 cup diced orange sections
    ½ cup flaked coconut

Combine crumbs and butter; reserve ⅓ cup for topping. Press remaining crumb mixture into an 8x8x2-inch baking dish.

Drain pineapple, reserving syrup. Dissolve gelatin and sugar in hot water. Stir in reserved syrup. Chill till partially set. Add sour cream and vanilla; whip till fluffy. Fold in the pineapple, oranges, and coconut; pour over crumbs in dish. Sprinkle top with reserved crumbs. Chill till firm. Cut in squares. Trim with maraschino cherries. Makes 9 servings.

Schaum Torte

It's heavenly! Meringue's marshmallow-y underneath, crisp on top—put together with a fluff of whipped cream, juicy sliced strawberries!—

6 egg whites
2 teaspoons lemon juice
1 teaspoon vanilla
½ teaspoon cream of tartar
¼ teaspoon salt
2 cups sugar

• • •

1½ cups whipping cream, whipped
1 pint fresh strawberries, sliced and
   lightly sweetened, if desired

Have egg whites at room temperature. Add lemon juice, vanilla, cream of tartar, and salt. Beat till frothy. Gradually add sugar, a small amount at a time, beating till very stiff peaks form and sugar is dissolved. Lightly butter a 9-inch spring-form pan. Spoon in meringue; spread evenly. Bake in very slow oven (275°) 2 hours. Cool; carefully remove from pan. Slice or break off top crust; set aside.

Spread about ⅓ of the whipped cream over bottom layer of torte; top with half the berries. Replace top crust; cover with remaining whipped cream and berries. Cut in wedges. Makes 8 to 10 servings.

Chocolate Torte Royale

1 6-ounce package (1 cup) semisweet
   chocolate pieces
Cinnamon Meringue Shell
2 beaten egg yolks
¼ cup water
1 cup whipping cream
¼ cup sugar
¼ teaspoon cinnamon

Melt the chocolate over *hot, not boiling* water. Cool slightly, then spread 2 tablespoons of the chocolate over bottom of cooled Cinnamon Meringue Shell.

To remaining chocolate, add egg yolks and water; blend. Chill till mixture is thick. Combine cream, sugar and cinnamon; whip till stiff. Spread *half* over chocolate in shell; fold remainder into chocolate mixture and spread on top.

Chill several hours or overnight. Garnish with whipped cream and sliced pecans. Makes 8 to 10 servings.

Cinnamon Meringue Shell

Cover a cooky sheet with a piece of heavy paper; draw an 8-inch circle in center. Beat 2 egg whites with ¼ teaspoon salt and ½ teaspoon vinegar till soft peaks form.

Blend ½ cup sugar and ¼ teaspoon cinnamon; gradually add to egg whites, beating till very stiff peaks form and all sugar has dissolved. Spread with circle—make bottom ½ inch thick and mound around edge, making it 1¾ inches high. Swirl ridges on outside of shell with back of teaspoon.

Bake in very slow oven (275°) for 1 hour. Turn off heat; let dry in oven (door closed) about 2 hours. Peel off paper.

Ribbon Alaska Pie

A spectacular! See it on page 4—

Fudge Sauce:
2 tablespoons butter
2 1-ounce squares unsweetened
   chocolate
1 cup sugar
1 6-ounce can (⅔ cup) evaporated milk
1 teaspoon vanilla

• • •

2 pints peppermint ice cream, softened
1 9-inch baked pastry shell

• • •

Meringue:
3 egg whites
½ teaspoon vanilla
¼ teaspoon cream of tartar
6 tablespoons sugar
¼ cup crushed peppermint-stick candy

Make Fudge Sauce: Mix butter, chocolate, cup sugar, and evaporated milk in saucepan; cook and stir over low heat till thick and blended. Remove from heat. Add 1 teaspoon vanilla. Cool; then chill.

Spread *1 pint* ice cream in pastry shell; cover with *half* the cooled Fudge Sauce; freeze. Repeat layers; freeze *firm*.

Prepare Meringue: Beat egg whites with ½ teaspoon vanilla and the cream of tartar till soft peaks form. Gradually add 6 tablespoons sugar, beating till stiff.

Reserve 1 tablespoon candy; fold remainder into meringue. Spread over pie, sealing to edges. Top with reserved candy. Bake in very hot oven (450°) about 3 minutes or till lightly browned. Serve at once or freeze.

Cheesecake Pie

1¼ cups plain- or cinnamon-graham-
  cracker crumbs
¼ cup butter or margarine, melted
1 8-ounce package cream cheese,
  softened
½ cup sugar
1 tablespoon lemon juice
½ teaspoon vanilla
Dash salt
2 eggs
1 cup dairy sour cream
2 tablespoons sugar
½ teaspoon vanilla

Mix crumbs and butter; press into buttered 8-inch pie plate, building up sides.

To make filling, beat cream cheese until fluffy; gradually blend in ½ cup sugar, the lemon juice, vanilla, and salt. Add eggs, one at a time, beating well after each. Pour filling into crumb crust. Bake in slow oven (325°) 25 to 30 minutes or till set.

Combine remaining ingredients and spoon atop pie. Bake 10 minutes more. Cool. Chill several hours. Serve with sweetened strawberries or Raspberry Sauce.

Raspberry Sauce

Thaw and crush one 10-ounce package frozen raspberries. Thoroughly mix in 2 teaspoons cornstarch. Add ½ cup currant jelly. Bring to boiling. Cook and stir till mixture thickens slightly. Strain; cool.

Candy-crust Mint Pie

1 6-ounce package (1 cup) semisweet
  chocolate pieces
3 tablespoons butter or margarine
2 cups crisp rice cereal
1 quart green mint ice cream,
  slightly softened
1 1-ounce square unsweetened
  chocolate, shaved

Melt chocolate and butter over hot water, stirring. Add cereal; mix. Press into unbuttered 9-inch pie plate; chill firm.

Let crust stand at room temperature 5 minutes; fill with alternating layers of ice cream and shaved chocolate. Serve at once. (Or freeze filled pie; let stand at room temperature 10 to 15 minutes; serve.)

Cheesecake Pie — terrific!

And it's the easiest cheesecake you ever made! The cream-cheese filling is rich and smooth, topper is tangy sour cream. Serve with strawberries or Raspberry Sauce.

Dramatic cake desserts

Angel Custard Royale

1 10-inch angel cake
6 beaten egg yolks
1½ cups sugar
¾ cup lemon juice
1½ teaspoons grated lemon peel
1 tablespoon unflavored gelatin
¼ cup water
6 egg whites

Trim crusts; tear cake into 1½- to 2-inch pieces. Combine yolks, ¾ *cup* of the sugar, lemon juice and peel. Cook over *hot, not boiling*, water until mixture coats spoon. Remove from heat; add gelatin softened in cold water. Stir till gelatin dissolves. Chill until partially set. Beat egg whites to soft peaks; gradually add remaining ¾ cup sugar, beating to stiff peaks. Fold into gelatin mixture. Add few drops yellow food coloring.

Arrange ⅓ of cake pieces loosely in bottom of 10-inch tube pan. Pour ⅓ of custard mixture over cake. Repeat twice.

Chill until firm. Invert on platter. Fill center with whipped cream. Serves 12.

Lemon Ladyfinger Torte

1½ cups sifted confectioners' sugar
½ cup soft butter
2 eggs
2 teaspoons grated lemon peel
2½ to 3 tablespoons lemon juice
4 dozen 4-inch-long single ladyfingers
1 cup whipping cream, whipped

Gradually add sugar to butter, creaming at medium speed on mixer till light and fluffy. Add eggs, one at a time, beating well after each. Gradually add peel and juice. (Mixture may look curdled.) Beat at high speed till smooth, about 10 minutes.

On cake plate, place 12 single ladyfingers, curved side down, in 2 rows; top with a *third* of the lemon mixture, then a layer of ladyfingers. Continue layers, ending with ladyfingers. Frost with sweetened whipped cream. Chill overnight. Makes 12 to 16 servings.

Easy Raspberry Ring

1 3-ounce package raspberry-flavored gelatin
Dash salt
1¼ cups boiling water
1 10-ounce package frozen raspberries
1 cup whipping cream, whipped
1 10x4x2-inch loaf angel cake

Dissolve gelatin and salt in boiling water. Add frozen raspberries and stir till thawed. Chill till partially set. Whip till fluffy; fold in whipped cream.

Rub brown crumbs from angel cake; tear cake in 1½- to 2-inch pieces. Loosely arrange half of cake in bottom of 10-inch tube pan. Pour half of gelatin over. Repeat. Chill firm. Unmold. Serves 8.

Marble Angel Ring

½ cup sugar
1 envelope (1 tablespoon) unflavored gelatin
¼ teaspoon salt
1¼ cups milk
2 1-ounce squares unsweetened chocolate
3 beaten egg yolks
1 teaspoon vanilla
3 egg whites
¼ cup sugar
1 cup whipping cream, whipped
1 10- or 10½-ounce loaf angel cake

Thoroughly mix ½ cup sugar, the gelatin, and salt. Add milk and chocolate. Heat and stir over low heat till chocolate melts and gelatin dissolves. Gradually add to yolks, mixing well. Add vanilla. Chill, stirring occasionally, till partially set.

Beat egg whites till soft peaks form; gradually add ¼ cup sugar, beating till stiff peaks form. Fold in chocolate mixture, then the whipped cream.

Remove brown crumbs from cake; tear cake in bite-size pieces; fold into chocolate mixture. Turn into 9-inch spring-form pan. Chill several hours or overnight. Unmold. Trim with whipped cream. Serves 10.

Almond-Brittle Cake

1½ cups sugar
1 teaspoon instant coffee
¼ cup corn syrup
¼ cup water
1 tablespoon sifted soda

. . .

2 cups whipping cream
1 to 2 tablespoons sugar
2 teaspoons vanilla
1 10-inch tube chocolate-angel cake
½ cup blanched almonds,
    halved and toasted

In saucepan, mix 1½ cups sugar, the instant coffee, corn syrup, and water. Cook to hard-crack stage (285° to 290°). Remove from heat; add soda at once.

Stir vigorously only till mixture blends and pulls away from sides of pan. Quickly pour foamy mixture into buttered 9x9x2-inch pan. (*Do not spread or stir.*) Cool; tap bottom of pan to remove candy. Crush in coarse crumbs.

Whip cream; stir in sugar and vanilla; add candy crumbs. Split angel cake in 3 layers; frost with whipped-cream mixture. Chill. Trim with toasted almonds.

Coffee-Toffee Torte

1 package angel-cake mix

. . .

1 package chocolate pudding
1 to 1½ tablespoons instant coffee
1 cup whipping cream, whipped

. . .

2 ¾-ounce chocolate-coated English
    toffee bars, chilled and crushed

Prepare angel-cake mix and bake in 10-inch tube pan according to package directions. Invert and cool thoroughly.

In saucepan, mix pudding and instant coffee. Prepare pudding following package directions, *but using only 1⅓ cups milk.* Cool. Beat until mixture is smooth; fold in *half* of the whipped cream.

Split cake in 3 layers. Divide pudding-cream mixture in half; use one half to spread between layers.

For the frosting, fold remaining whipped cream into remaining pudding mixture; use to frost top and sides of cake. Sprinkle frosted cake with crushed toffee bars. Chill till serving time. Makes 12 servings.

Chocolate Angel Layers

Prepare 1 package angel-cake mix sifting ¼ cup cocoa (regular-type, dry) and 1 tablespoon instant coffee powder with flour mixture. Bake using package directions. Cool; cut crosswise in 3 even layers. Spread Milk-chocolate Frosting between layers, on sides, and top. Chill till set.

Milk-chocolate Frosting: In top of double boiler, place one 6-ounce package semisweet chocolate pieces *or* six 1-ounce squares semisweet chocolate, ¼ pound marshmallows, and ½ cup milk.

Heat over simmering water till chocolate melts and mixture blends; stir occasionally. Chill. Stir till smooth. Whip 1 cup whipping cream; fold in. Makes 3 cups.

Chocolate-fleck Cake

1 package yellow- or white-cake mix
⅛ cup chocolate shot
1½ cups whipping cream
⅔ cup instant cocoa (dry)
¼ cup finely chopped pecans

Mix batter from cake mix according to package directions; fold in chocolate shot. Bake in 2 paper-lined 8x1½-inch round pans as directed on package.

For the frosting, combine whipping cream and instant cocoa; chill, then whip till fluffy. Frost cooled cake, sprinkling nuts between layers. Chill till serving time.

Almond Fluff Layers

1 package angel-cake mix
¼ cup cocoa (regular-type, dry)
1 6-ounce package (1 cup) semisweet
    chocolate pieces
1 cup blanched almonds, halved
    and toasted
2 cups whipping cream, whipped

Prepare cake mix using package directions, sifting cocoa with flour mixture. Bake as directed on package. Cool; cut crosswise in 3 even layers.

Melt chocolate in top of double boiler over *hot, not boiling,* water. Cool to room temperature. Fold chocolate and almonds into whipped cream, allowing chocolate to harden in flecks. Spread between cake layers, then frost top and sides. Serves 12.

Easy Chocolate-Nut Tarts   Frilly pastry shells get a coating of chocolate and nuts, delicious filling—peppermint-stick ice cream. (You fashion the shells with foil—no tart pans to wash!)

Impressive in a shell!

Chocolate-Nut Tarts

Plain pastry
8 5-inch circles heavy-duty foil

. . .

1 6-ounce package (1 cup) semisweet
  chocolate pieces, melted
⅓ cup chopped blanched almonds,
  toasted
1 quart peppermint-stick ice cream
Semisweet chocolate curls

Use pastry recipe calling for 1½ cups flour;* roll to ⅛ inch. Cut in eight 5-inch circles; prick with fork. Lightly press each atop a foil circle. Holding pastry and foil together, shape in tarts by fluting edges. Bake on cooky sheet in very hot oven (450°) about 10 minutes or till done. Cool on rack. Remove foil.

Spread bottom and sides of each tart with melted chocolate; sprinkle almonds over. Cool. At serving time, fill with scoops of ice cream. Trim with cocolate curls.

  *Or use 1 stick pastry mix.

Lacy Almond Desserts

½ cup butter or margarine, melted
½ cup sugar
3 tablespoons all-purpose flour
2 tablespoons milk
¾ cup blanched almonds,
  very finely chopped
Brick vanilla ice cream
Hot fudge sauce

Combine first 5 ingredients; blend. Drop by level tablespoons, one or two at a time onto *very-well-greased* cooky sheet.

Bake at 350° till circles are golden brown, about 7 to 10 minutes. Cool 1 to 2 minutes or till edges are firm enough to lift with a thin spatula. Loosen circles carefully, but quickly. Remove to rack; cool. Repeat till all batter is used. (Stir occasionally.) Makes about 20 lacy circles.

To serve, sandwich a quarter-pint slice of ice cream between each 2 circles. Spoon fudge sauce atop. Serves about 10, depending on the number of circles you have.

Cream Puffs

½ cup butter or margarine
1 cup boiling water

• • •

1 cup sifted all-purpose flour
¼ teaspoon salt
4 eggs

• • •

1 recipe French Custard Filling
1 recipe Chocolate Sauce

Melt butter in boiling water. Add flour and salt all at once; stir vigorously. Cook, stirring constantly, till mixture pulls away from sides of pan and forms a ball that doesn't separate. Remove from heat and cool slightly. Add eggs, one at a time, beating vigorously after each until smooth.

Drop dough by heaping tablespoons 3 inches apart on greased cooky sheet.

Bake in very hot oven (450°) 15 minutes, then in slow oven (325°) 25 minutes. Remove cream puffs from oven; split. Turn oven *off* and put cream puffs back in oven to dry out, about 20 minutes. Cool on rack.

Just before serving, fill centers with French Custard Filling. Replace tops; drizzle with Chocolate Sauce. Sprinkle chopped nuts atop. Makes 10 big puffs.

French Custard Filling

A luscious way to fill a cream puff! Another time, try ice cream or packaged pudding—

⅔ cup sugar
2 tablespoons all-purpose flour
2 tablespoons cornstarch
½ teaspoon salt

• • •

3 cups milk
2 beaten egg yolks
2 teaspoons vanilla
1 cup whipping cream, whipped

Combine sugar, flour, cornstarch, and salt. Gradually stir in milk. Cook and stir till mixture thickens and boils; cook and stir 2 to 3 minutes longer. Stir a little of hot mixture into egg yolk; return to hot mixture. Stirring constantly, bring just to boiling. Add vanilla.

Cover entire surface with clear plastic wrap or waxed paper; cool. Beat smooth; fold in whipped cream. Makes about 1 quart.

Chocolate Sauce (*for Cream Puffs*)

1 cup sugar
¾ cup water
½ cup light corn syrup
3 1-ounce squares unsweetened
    chocolate, melted
1 teaspoon vanilla

In saucepan combine sugar, water, and syrup; bring to a boil. Gradually add to chocolate, blending well. Boil gently 10 to 15 minutes, stirring occasionally. Add vanilla. Cover entire surface with clear plastic wrap; cool. Makes about 1⅔ cups.

Elegant Eclairs

Mix batter as directed for Cream Puffs. Put mixture through a pastry tube or paper cone, making 4-inch strips, ¾ inch wide, on greased cooky sheet.

Bake as for Cream Puffs. Frost with Chocolate Icing. Fill with French Custard Filling before serving. Makes about 14.

Chocolate Icing (*for Eclairs*)

Melt two 1-ounce squares unsweetened chocolate and 1½ tablespoons butter in top of double boiler. Remove from heat.

Stir in ⅔ cup sifted confectioners' sugar and 2 tablespoons milk, blending till mixture is smooth and of spreading consistency. Spread on tops of eclairs.

Chocolate Dessert Cups

1 7-ounce package solid chocolate-mint
    candy wafers, *or* 1 6-ounce package
    (1 cup) semisweet chocolate pieces
2 tablespoons shortening
Peppermint-stick, chocolate, vanilla,
    or coffee ice cream

Melt chocolate over *hot, not boiling* water, stirring till smooth. Cool to room temperature. Place 8 paper bake cups in muffin pans. With a teaspoon, swirl chocolate mixture around inside of each cup, covering entire surface with a thin layer of chocolate. Chill.

When chocolate cups harden, *carefully* tear off paper. Fill with scoops of ice cream. Top each with a chocolate wafer.

You're

No nicer way to let your hospitality shine—ask friends in for a tea! Plan a pretty table, give the food a party flair. The next 12 pages show you how!

invited for tea!

How to set the tea table
Perfect tea and coffee
Party-going punch
Fancy teatime sandwiches
Cookies for company
Elegant little extras

How to set a tea table— or tea tray

Tea tray, all set for a party

For an informal afternoon tea, choose a pleasant spot—in front of the fireplace or on the porch or patio. Before guests arrive, set the tea tray and place it on a convenient table. Tea tray holds tea, hot water, cream, sugar, and lemon. Cups and saucers go at back and side of tray, or near by on table. Spoons are next. Stack napkins between plates, or arrange. (Use plates large enough to hold cup, saucer, plus a snack. Or you may use smaller plates and no saucers.) If knives and forks are needed, arrange them on the tray.

Just before serving, fill container with *boiling* water and teapot with freshly brewed tea. (You may want to use a concentrated brew.) Pour tea; then, as guests request, dilute with hot water, add sugar, cream (really milk), and lemon. Guests help themselves to simple snacks (could be fork desserts) placed near by.

A more formal tea usually honors someone—a speaker, a new neighbor, club visitors.

Before the day of the tea, ask a friend to pour. You'll be free to make guests feel at home and replenish tea and food.

Gleaming silver, exquisite china, dainty food, and a pretty centerpiece will make a beautiful table. Suit the setting to the table, the room, the number of guests.

You may serve from only one side of the table or offer beverages at only one end.

However, when your tea is a big affair, it's a good idea to set the tea table for "two-way travel." Place similar plates of tea dainties on both sides of the table; offer a beverage at each end. Guests preferring coffee, punch, or chocolate take one side; tea fans take the other.

Person pouring hands beverage to guests, who help themselves to other refreshments. They may stand or sit down to eat.

Formal tea table—use silver and pretty china, duplicate service

Perfect tea and coffee

Perfect Hot Tea

Black tea, green tea, oolong, and exotic perfumed teas differ only in processing. They may come from the same tea plant and are brewed in the same way.

Use 1 teaspoon tea or 1 tea bag for each cup. Place tea in teapot heated by rinsing with boiling water. Bring freshly drawn cold water to a bubbling boil; immediately pour over tea. Steep tea 5 minutes. Give tea a stir and serve at once.

If you like a weak brew, dilute tea with a little hot water. Pass sugar, lemon, milk.

In a hurry? Use instant tea.

Tea Concentrate

When you're planning a large formal tea, it's handy to make tea concentrate ahead. Then at teatime, you simply pour a little concentrate into each cup and fill with hot, hot water. The tea can be strong or weak—depending on the amount of concentrate you use each time.

Or, just before serving, combine concentrate with hot water in a large teapot—1 cup concentrate to 6 cups boiling water.

Tea Concentrate for 40 to 45 servings: Bring to a high bubbling boil 6 cups freshly drawn cold water. Remove from heat and promptly add ¼ pound loose tea, stirring in leaves. Cover; steep 5 minutes. Strain into teapot and set aside.

Concentrate cloudy? Adding the hot water at teatime will make it sparkle again.

Iced Tea

To make 4 glasses of iced tea, measure 2 tablespoons tea or 6 tea bags into teapot. Pour 2 cups fresh, vigorously boiling water over the leaves. Cover and let tea stand 5 minutes; stir. Then pour brew through a tea strainer into a pitcher. Immediately add 2 cups cold water and let tea cool at room temperature till serving time.

Pour tea into tall ice-filled glasses. Offer juicy lemon wedges and sugar.

Coffee

Whatever the style of your coffeepot or coffee maker and your individual coffee preference, you're bound to pour a good cup every time if you follow these few "golden rules":
- Start with a thoroughly clean coffee maker, scrubbed, sudsed, rinsed, dried.
- Use fresh, cold water *and* fresh coffee (store in airtight container; keep cool).
- Get the right grind coffee for your coffee maker or coffeepot.
- Measure coffee. Allow 2 level tablespoons coffee (or 1 coffee measure) for each ¾ cup water, *or* determine the proportions that best suit your individual taste, brand of coffee, and coffee maker. *For a crowd*, one pound makes 50 cups.
- Bring water to a full rolling boil before it comes in contact with the coffee.
- After coffee's made, don't let it boil. You lose the good flavor of the brew.

Instant Coffee for a Few Friends

For each cup needed, place 1 rounded teaspoon instant coffee and ¾ measuring cup boiling water in coffeepot. Heat over *low* heat 5 minutes. For just a few, it's easier to fix coffee right in the cups.

Instant Coffee for a Party

Empty a 2-ounce jar instant coffee into a large kettle; add about 5 quarts boiling water. Stir, then cover several minutes. Do not boil. Makes 25 servings.

Iced Coffee

Make coffee double strength, using half the amount of water for the usual amount of coffee. Pour hot into tall ice-filled tumblers. Pass confectioners' sugar.

Or, use instant coffee: Use double the amount you would use for a cup. Dissolve in ½ glass cold water; fill with ice; stir.

Party-going punches

Raspberry-Mint Punch

¼ cup sugar
½ cup slightly packed fresh mint
 leaves
1 cup *boiling* water
1 10-ounce package frozen red
 raspberries
1 6-ounce can frozen lemonade
 concentrate
2 cups cold water

Combine first 3 ingredients; let stand 5 minutes. Add berries and concentrate; stir till thawed. Strain into chilled pitcher half full of ice; add cold water, stir. Garnish glasses with fresh mint. Serves 8.

Grand Glorious Punch

Dissolve one 3-ounce package cherry-flavored gelatin in 1 cup *boiling* water. Stir in one 6-ounce can frozen lemonade *or* pineapple-orange juice concentrate. Add 3 cups cold water and one 1-quart bottle cranberry juice cocktail, chilled.

In a large punch bowl place two trays of ice cubes or a molded ice ring. Pour punch over ice. Slowly pour in one 1-pint 12-ounce bottle ginger ale, chilled. Fruit-flavored sherbet may be added if desired. Makes about 25 servings.

Pineapple-Lime Cooler

1 envelope lemon-lime flavored
 drink powder
¾ cup sugar
4 cups cold water
1 can (2¼ cups) unsweetened
 pineapple juice, chilled
½ cup lime juice, chilled
1 lime, thinly sliced

Combine ingredients, chill. Serve over ice, or float Pineapple Ice Ring. Serves 10.

Pineapple Ice Ring: Arrange halved canned pineapple rings scallop-fashion in bottom of ring mold. Tuck in mint sprigs between scallops. Add water to cover pineapple; freeze. Fill mold with water; freeze.

Ginger-Lime Punch

Sparkling, "barely green"—with flavor zingo that's a real surprise!—

2 6-ounce cans frozen limeade
 concentrate
1 6-ounce can frozen lemonade
 concentrate
1 tablespoon chopped candied ginger
4 cups cold water
1 large bottle (3½ to 4 cups) ginger
 ale, chilled

Pour concentrates into punch bowl. Add ginger; chill at least 2 hours to blend flavors. Add cold water and ice. Pour ginger ale down side of bowl. Trim with Citrus Floaters: Stack fluted lemon slice, small lime slice, and mint sprig. Serves 20.

Golden Sherbet Punch

2 cups sugar
1½ cups fresh mint leaves
2 cups boiling water
¾ cup lemon juice
1 12-ounce can (1½ cups) apricot
 nectar, chilled
1 6-ounce can *each* frozen
 limeade concentrate,
 orange-juice concentrate,
 and pineapple-juice concentrate
2 large bottles (7 to 8 cups)
 ginger ale, chilled
1 quart lemon sherbet

Combine sugar, mint, and boiling water; stir to dissolve sugar. Cool. Chill. Strain into chilled punch bowl. Add lemon juice, apricot nectar, concentrates. Pour ginger ale down side of bowl. Top with scoops of sherbet. Trim with mint. Serves 20 to 25.

Hawaiian Lemonade

Combine one 6-ounce can frozen lemonade concentrate with *1 can water;* add one 12-ounce can *each* chilled apricot nectar and unsweetened pineapple juice. Add ice. Pour in 1 small bottle chilled ginger ale.

Spicy Harvest Punch

Tea Base, cooled
1 pint bottle cranberry-juice cocktail
1½ cups water
½ cup orange juice
⅓ cup lemon juice, few lemon slices

Combine ingredients. Chill. Serves 6 to 8.
  Tea Base: Pour 2½ cups boiling water over 2 tablespoons tea and ¼ teaspoon *each* allspice, cinnamon, nutmeg. Cover; steep 5 minutes. Strain. Add ¾ cup sugar.

Trader's Punch

2 cups orange juice
2 cups lemon juice
1 cup grenadine syrup
½ cup light corn syrup
2½ quarts ginger ale, chilled
Lemon or other fresh fruit, sliced

Combine orange juice, lemon juice, and syrups; pour over block of ice to chill. Just before serving, pour ginger ale down side of bowl. Add fruit. Makes 4 quarts.

Cool punch, tiny sandwiches

It's an occasion when you pass trays of dainty sandwiches like these and offer refreshing cups of Trader's Punch as the go-with.

Fancy sandwiches

Miniature Flowerpots

Unsliced enriched bread
1 6½- or 7½-ounce can (1 cup) crab
  meat, flaked
½ cup finely chopped celery
¼ cup finely chopped green pepper
¼ teaspoon salt
1 tablespoon lemon juice
⅓ cup mayonnaise or salad dressing

Cut bread in 1-inch slices; freeze. Cut out
circles from frozen slices with 1-inch round
cutter. Hollow out centers with scissors or
knife, leaving bottom and sides about ¼
inch thick. Combine next 4 ingredients,
dash pepper. Add lemon juice, mayonnaise; mix. Chill. Heap filling in "flowerpots." Top with parsley.

Sandwich Bars

1 cup finely grated carrots
½ cup chopped ripe olives
¼ cup minced celery
1½ tablespoons minced onion
¼ teaspoon salt
¼ cup mayonnaise or salad dressing
5 slices enriched sandwich bread
5 slices whole-wheat sandwich bread

Combine first 6 ingredients, chill. Spread
on white bread; top with whole-wheat.
Trim off crusts; cut sandwiches in thirds.
Trim with fans of ripe-olive strips.

Jigsaw Sandwiches

1 3-ounce package cream cheese
1 tablespoon milk
1 teaspoon Worcestershire sauce
4 to 5 slices crisp-cooked bacon,
  crumbled
Sliced enriched sandwich loaf
Sliced whole-wheat sandwich loaf

Soften cream cheese and blend in milk and
Worcestershire. Add bacon. Cut breads in
2-inch rounds with cooky cutter. Spread
half of rounds (equal number white and
whole-wheat bread) with cheese mixture.

Divide the remaining rounds in three
groups, each with an equal number of light
and dark rounds. Use one group each for
Double Rounds, Stripes, Checkerboards.

Double Rounds: With hole of doughnut
cutter, cut tiny circles from center of
rounds. Fit the tiny whole-wheat circles in
the holes of large white ones and vice versa.

Stripes: Cut rounds in three strips, making center strip widest. Fit together, alternating white and whole-wheat strips; hold
together with bits of filling.

Checkerboards: Cut rounds in fourths.
Make checkerboards of white and whole
wheat, spreading small amount of cheese
on edges to hold together.

Note: For good-looking sandwiches with
smooth edges, freeze bread first, then cut
while frozen.

Miniature Flowerpots are tiny cups filled
with crab salad, trimmed with parsley "blos-
soms." Arrange with tasty Sandwich Bars.

Jigsaw Sandwiches offer all-in-fun top decks
—checkerboards, circles, and stripes. Below
deck—a luscious cheese-bacon filling.

Ham Pinwheels

These appear on the tea table, page 49—

1 cup ground cooked ham
1 3-ounce package cream cheese,
  softened
1 teaspoon horseradish
2 tablespoons mayonnaise or
  salad dressing

• • •

1 unsliced enriched sandwich loaf,
  sliced ¼ inch thick lengthwise*
Soft butter or margarine
Stuffed green olives

Blend first 4 ingredients. Trim crusts from bread slices. Spread each slice lightly with butter, then with 3 tablespoons of the ham mixture; line up olives at narrow end; roll bread as for jellyroll. Seal end with small amount soft butter. Wrap and chill, *seam side* down. To serve, unwrap and cut ½-inch slices. Makes about 42.

*Ask your bakery to do the slicing.

Pepper Pinwheels

1 unsliced enriched sandwich loaf,
  sliced ¼ inch thick lengthwise*
1 5-ounce jar pimento-cheese spread
1 medium green pepper, cut in
  ⅛-inch strips

Trim crusts from bread slices; spread each with pimento-cheese spread. Place strips of green pepper across each bread slice at 1-inch intervals. Beginning at narrow end, roll as for jellyroll. Wrap and chill. At serving time, cut in ⅜-inch slices.

*Ask your bakery to do the slicing.

Pinwheels are always pretty on a tea tray. Here Pepper Pinwheels go round in pimento-cheese circles, with green-pepper flecks.

Water Cress Roll-ups

14 slices enriched sandwich bread
1 5-ounce jar pineapple-cheese spread
¼ cup chopped water cress
Tiny sprigs of water cress

Trim crusts from bread slices. Pat gently to flatten. Spread each slice with about 2 teaspoons cheese spread. Sprinkle with chopped water cress. Roll up as for jelly-roll; anchor with toothpicks. Place *seam side* down on cooky sheet. Cover and chill till serving time.

At serving time, remove toothpicks. Tuck sprig of water cress in one end of each roll-up. Makes 14 sandwiches.

Water Cress Canape Sandwiches: Trim crusts from slices of enriched sandwich bread. Spread with pineapple-cheese spread; cut each slice in fourths. Chill. Center tiny water-cress sprig on each dainty sandwich.

Date-roll Ginger Snips

1 3-ounce package cream cheese,
  softened
1 tablespoon milk
2 tablespoons very finely chopped
  candied ginger
1 can date-nut roll

Blend cream cheese and milk. Add candied ginger. Slice date-nut roll about ¾ inch thick. Spread half the slices with cream-cheese mixture. Top with remaining slices. Cut a crescent from one side of each sandwich. Part remaining will be a petal-shaped sandwich—see picture below.

Date-roll Ginger Snips are filled with spicy candied ginger and cream cheese. Date-nut roll from a can makes these quick as a wink.

Shrimp Luncheon Sandwiches

1 3-ounce package cream cheese,
    softened
2 tablespoons mayonnaise
1 tablespoon catsup
1 teaspoon prepared mustard
Dash garlic powder
1 cup chopped canned or cooked
    cleaned shrimp
¼ cup finely chopped celery
1 teaspoon finely chopped onion
10 slices lightly buttered
    sandwich bread

Blend cheese with mayonnaise; mix in catsup, mustard, and garlic powder. Stir in shrimp, celery, and onion. Use as a filling between slices of sandwich bread. Trim crusts, if desired. Cut each diagonally into 4 triangles. Makes 20 tea sandwiches.

Easy Sandwich Loaf

Egg Filling:

3 hard-cooked eggs, chopped
3 tablespoons finely chopped onion
2 tablespoons chopped stuffed olives
2 tablespoons mayonnaise
1 teaspoon prepared mustard
¼ teaspoon salt

Deviled-ham Filling:

1 2¼-ounce can deviled ham
2 tablespoons finely chopped celery
1 tablespoon finely chopped
    green pepper
1 teaspoon prepared horseradish

• • •

8 slices enriched bread
Soft butter or margarine
2 3-ounce packages cream cheese
1½ tablespoons mayonnaise

Combine ingredients for fillings. Trim crusts from bread; butter. Arrange 2 slices, butter side up, with narrow ends *touching.* Spread with *half* the Egg Filling. Top with 2 slices bread. Spread with Deviled-ham Filling. Top with 2 more bread slices; spread with remaining Egg Filling. Top with last 2 bread slices, butter side down. Wrap loaf in foil; chill.

Soften cream cheese, blend with 1½ tablespoons mayonnaise, beat till fluffy. Frost loaf; chill. Trim with stuffed-olive slices parsley. Cut in 6 or 7 1-inch slices.

Frosted Ribbon Loaf

Ham Filling:

1 cup ground cooked ham
⅓ cup finely chopped celery
2 tablespoons drained pickle relish
½ teaspoon horseradish
¼ cup mayonnaise

Egg Filling:

4 hard-cooked eggs, chopped
⅓ cup chopped stuffed green olives
2 tablespoons finely chopped
    green onion
2 teaspoons prepared mustard
¼ cup mayonnaise

• • •

Unsliced sandwich loaf
4 3-ounce packages cream cheese,
    softened
⅓ cup milk

Ham Filling: Combine first 5 ingredients. *Egg Filling:* Combine next 5 ingredients. Trim crusts from loaf. Slice bread lengthwise in 3 equal layers; butter slices. Spread first slice, buttered side up, with ham filling, second slice with egg filling; end with third slice. Wrap in foil and chill.

At serving time,* beat cream cheese with milk till fluffy. Frost top and sides of loaf. Sprinkle generously with snipped parsley. Makes 10 slices.

*Or, frost early, cover loosely, and store in refrigerator till serving time.

Little Ribbon Triangles

Prepare Ham Filling and Egg Filling as for Frosted Ribbon Loaf.

Trim crusts from 6 slices whole-wheat and 6 slices enriched white bread. Butter one side of each slice. Spread 3 slices white bread with Ham Filling. Top each with slice of whole-wheat, buttered side down; spread with ⅓ cup cream cheese with chives; top with white bread, buttered side down, and spread with Egg Filling. Top with whole-wheat, butter side down. Wrap sandwiches tightly in foil; chill.

To one 8-ounce package softened cream cheese, gradually add ¼ cup milk and beat fluffy. Cut sandwiches diagonally and spread tops and sides (except diagonal) with cream-cheese mixture. Makes 6.

Frosted Ribbon Loaf

It's strictly for company and simply delicious! You slice through the luscious cream-cheese frosting to reveal pretty layers of ham and egg filling. Tomato rose is fitting trim.

Party Sandwich Filling

1 8-ounce package cream cheese, softened
¾ cup chopped California walnuts or pecans
¼ cup chopped green pepper
¼ cup chopped onion
3 tablespoons chopped pimiento
1 tablespoon catsup
3 hard-cooked eggs, finely chopped
¾ teaspoon salt
Dash pepper

Combine all ingredients. Use as a filling between lightly buttered slices of sandwich bread. Trim crusts, if desired. Cut each sandwich diagonally in 4 triangles. Makes 2⅓ cups sandwich filling—enough for about 8 large sandwiches (32 little triangles).

Cream Cheese-Bacon Bars

1 3-ounce package cream cheese
1 tablespoon milk
4 slices crisp-cooked bacon, crumbled
1 teaspoon horseradish
½ teaspoon Worcestershire sauce
12 slices sandwich bread

Soften cream cheese. Add remaining ingredients except bread, blending well. Sandwich between bread slices. Trim crusts. Cut sandwiches in thirds (18 bars).

Nut-bread Sandwiches

Cut nut bread in thin slices. Sandwich with whipped cream cheese. Halve or cut in shapes. Trim crusts, if desired.

Cookies for company

Creme-filled Cookies

6 tablespoons chilled butter
1 cup sifted all-purpose flour
2½ tablespoons light cream
Almond Filling

With pastry blender, cut butter into flour till pieces are the size of small peas.

Sprinkle 1 tablespoon cream over part of the mixture; gently toss with fork, push to one side of bowl. Repeat till all is moistened. Gather up with fingers; form in ball. On lightly floured surface, roll to slightly less than ⅛ inch. Cut dough in rounds with a floured 1½-inch cutter.

Dip one side of each cooky in sugar. Place sugar side up, ½ inch apart, on an ungreased baking sheet. With fork, prick each cooky in 4 parallel rows.

Bake at 375° about 8 minutes or until golden brown and puffy. Remove at once to a cooling rack. When cookies are cool, sandwich with Almond Filling. Makes about 2½ dozen sandwiched cookies.

Almond Filling: Thoroughly combine ¾ cup sifted confectioners' sugar, 1 tablespoon soft butter, ⅛ teaspoon almond extract, and 1 tablespoon light cream, (or enough to make of spreading consistency).

Chocolate Meringues

2 egg whites
1 teaspoon vanilla
⅛ teaspoon salt
⅛ teaspoon cream of tartar
¾ cup sugar
1 6-ounce package (1 cup)
  semisweet chocolate pieces
¼ cup chopped California walnuts

Beat first 4 ingredients until soft peaks form. Add sugar gradually, beating till stiff peaks form. Fold in chocolate pieces and nuts. Cover cooky sheet with plain paper. Drop mixture by rounded teaspoons. Bake at 300° for 25 minutes. Cool slightly before removing from paper. Makes 24.

Cream-cheese Pastry

Let one 3-ounce package cream cheese and ½ cup butter soften at room temperature; blend. Stir in 1 cup sifted all-purpose flour and ¼ teaspoon salt.

Chill and use as directed below, in Teatime Tassies and Cherry Tarts.

Teatime Tassies

1 recipe Cream-cheese Pastry
1 egg
¾ cup brown sugar
1 tablespoon soft butter
  or margarine
1 teaspoon vanilla
Dash salt
⅔ cup coarsely broken pecans

Chill Cream-cheese Pastry about 1 hour. Shape in 2 dozen 1-inch balls; place in tiny ungreased 1¾-inch muffin cups. Press dough evenly against bottom and sides.

Beat together egg, sugar, butter, vanilla, and salt just till smooth. Divide *half* the pecans among pastry-lined cups; add egg mixture and top with remaining pecans. Bake in slow oven (325°) 25 minutes or till filling is set. Cool; remove from pans.

Cherry Tarts

1 recipe Cream-cheese Pastry
½ cup commercial cherry
  preserves, cut up
½ cup chopped California walnuts
1 teaspoon grated lemon peel

Chill Cream-cheese Pastry 3 to 4 hours. Mix preserves, nuts, and peel. Divide dough in half. On lightly floured surface, roll each half to 12x10-inch rectangle, ⅛ inch thick. Cut each in twenty 2½-inch squares. Place ½ teaspoon preserves in center of each square. Moisten edges; fold in triangles. Seal edges with fork. Bake on ungreased cooky sheet in moderate oven (375°) about 12 minutes. Dust with confectioners' sugar. Makes 40.

Cherry Chocolate Cookies

Each dainty cooky wears a crisp nut coating, a topknot of cherry preserves. These are fun for February, pretty anytime—just the thing to serve with fancy tea.

Cherry Chocolate Cookies

½ cup shortening
¼ cup brown sugar
½ teaspoon salt
1 egg yolk
1 1-ounce square unsweetened
   chocolate, melted
1 cup sifted all-purpose flour
· · ·
1 slightly beaten egg white
1 cup broken California walnuts
   or pecans
· · ·
⅓ cup cherry preserves

Cream together shortening, sugar, salt, and egg yolk till light and fluffy. Blend in chocolate. Stir in flour. Chill ½ hour.

Shape dough in 1-inch balls; dip in egg white and roll in nuts. Place 2½ inches apart on greased cooky sheet; press centers with thumb to indent.

Bake in moderate oven (350°) 8 minutes. Remove from oven; press centers again. (Hot! Use wood or metal handle.) Bake 8 minutes longer or till done. Cool slightly; remove from pan. Just before serving, fill centers with preserves. Makes 3 dozen.

Apricot Pastries

2 cups dried apricots
3 cups sifted all-purpose flour
1 tablespoon sugar
½ teaspoon salt
1 cup shortening
½ cup milk, scalded
1 package active dry yeast
1 slightly beaten egg
½ teaspoon vanilla

Simmer apricots in 2 cups water till tender. Cool. Sift together dry ingredients; cut in shortening till mixture resembles coarse crumbs. Cool hot milk to *warm;* add dry yeast and let soften. Add egg and vanilla. Add to flour mixture; mix well.

Divide dough in 4 parts. On surface well dusted with confectioners' sugar, roll one part at a time to 10-inch square. Cut each in sixteen 2½-inch squares; place heaping teaspoon of apricots in center of each. Pinch two opposite corners together. Place 2 inches apart on greased cooky sheet. Let stand 10 minutes. Bake at 350° for 10 to 12 minutes. Remove immediately from pan; roll in confectioners' sugar. Makes 64.

Bachelor's-buttons

A Neiman-Marcus teatime specialty—

¾ cup butter
1 cup brown sugar
1 egg
2 cups sifted all-purpose flour
1 teaspoon soda
¼ teaspoon ginger
¼ teaspoon cinnamon
¼ teaspoon salt
1 teaspoon vanilla
1 cup chopped nuts

Cream butter, add sugar gradually, and beat well. Add unbeaten egg. Sift together dry ingredients; stir into butter mixture. Fold in vanilla and nuts. Chill several hours for easy handling.

Make into small balls (1 level teaspoon dough for tiny cookies, 2 for medium). Dip balls in granulated sugar; place 2 inches apart on lightly greased cooky sheet, and press down with a fork. Bake at 375° until nicely browned, about 8 to 10 minutes. Makes 12 dozen tiny cookies.

Macaroon Top Hats

½ cup butter or margarine
½ cup sugar
1 egg
1 egg yolk
1 teaspoon grated lemon peel
1½ cups sifted all-purpose flour
½ teaspoon baking powder
¼ teaspoon salt
Almond Topper

Cream together butter and sugar until light and fluffy. Add egg and egg yolk (reserve egg white for Topper); beat well. Stir in peel. Sift together dry ingredients; add to creamed mixture, mixing well. Drop from tip of teaspoon, 2 inches apart, onto ungreased cooky sheet. With bottom of tumbler (first butter and dip in sugar), press each cooky down slightly till about 1½ inches in diameter.

Center each with dab of Almond Topper; trim with a toasted almond half. Bake in moderate oven (350°) 10 to 12 minutes or till lightly browned. Makes about 5 dozen.

Almond Topper: Beat 1 egg white with dash *each* salt and cinnamon to stiff peaks; gradually beat in ½ cup sugar. Fold in ½ cup chopped toasted almonds.

Pecan Dainties

1 egg white
Dash salt
1 cup light brown sugar
1½ cups pecan halves

Beat egg white with salt until soft peaks form. Add brown sugar in two additions, beating lightly after each. (Mixture will be much thinner than for meringue.) Stir in nuts and drop, 2 inches apart, from a teaspoon onto a greased cooky sheet. Bake in very slow oven (250°) about 30 minutes. Remove from cooky sheet immediately. Makes about 3½ dozen cookies.

Vanilla Wafers

½ cup soft butter or margarine
½ cup shortening
⅔ cup sugar
2 teaspoons vanilla
1 teaspoon salt
2 eggs
2¾ cups sifted all-purpose flour

Cream together butter, shortening, and sugar till fluffy. Add vanilla and salt. Add eggs, one at a time, beating well after each. Stir in flour. Mix well.

Drop from teaspoon onto greased cooky sheet. Flatten with *flat-bottomed* glass. Bake at 375° for 8 to 10 minutes or till delicately browned on edges. Remove immediately from pan. Makes about 7 dozen.

Frosty Date Balls

½ cup soft butter or margarine
⅓ cup sifted confectioners' sugar
1 tablespoon water
1 teaspoon vanilla
1¼ cups sifted all-purpose flour
Dash salt
⅔ cup chopped pitted dates
½ cup chopped California walnuts

Cream butter and sugar thoroughly. Stir in water and vanilla. Add flour and salt. Mix well. Stir in dates and nuts. Roll in 1-inch balls. Place 2½ inches apart on an ungreased baking sheet.

Bake in slow oven (300°) about 20 minutes, or till cookies are set but not brown. While warm, roll in confectioners' sugar. Makes 2½ dozen cookies.

Elegant little extras

Petits Fours

¼ cup butter or margarine
¼ cup shortening
1 cup sugar
½ teaspoon vanilla
¼ teaspoon almond extract
2 cups sifted cake flour
3 teaspoons baking powder
¼ teaspoon salt
¾ cup milk
¾ cup (6) egg whites
¼ cup sugar
1 recipe Petits Fours Glaze

Cream butter and shortening thoroughly. Gradually add 1 cup sugar, and cream together until light and fluffy. Add extracts. Sift together flour, baking powder, and salt; add to creamed mixture alternately with milk, beating after each addition. Beat egg whites until foamy; gradually add remaining ¼ cup sugar and beat until mixture forms soft peaks. Fold into batter. Bake in paper-lined 13x9x2-inch pan in moderate oven (350°) about 30 minutes.

Cool cake 5 minutes before removing from pan. Cut cooled cake in 1½-inch squares or in diamonds. Line up on rack with cooky sheet below. Spoon or pour Glaze evenly over cakes. (Keep glaze over hot water.) Makes about 40 little cakes.

Petits Fours Glaze

Cook 3 cups sugar, ¼ teaspoon cream of tartar, 1½ cups hot water to thin syrup (226°)*. Cool to lukewarm (110°). Add 1 teaspoon vanilla; gradually add sifted confectioners' sugar (about 2¼ cups) till icing is of consistency to pour. Tint with few drops food coloring, if desired. Spoon or pour icing evenly over cakes.

For pretty glaze, give cake two coats icing. (If icing gets too thick, add few drops hot water.) Pipe frosting rose on each cake or trim with candy decoration.

*If your candy thermometer doesn't register 212° when tested in boiling water, adjust recipe temperatures accordingly.

Date-Nut Loaf

1 8-ounce package pitted dates, cut up
2 tablespoons shortening
1 tablespoon shredded orange peel
½ cup fresh orange juice
1 beaten egg
2 cups sifted all-purpose flour
⅓ cup sugar
1 teaspoon baking powder
1 teaspoon soda
½ teaspoon salt
½ cup chopped walnuts

Pour ½ cup boiling water over dates and shortening; cool to room temperature. Add orange peel and juice; stir in egg. Sift together dry ingredients; add to mixture; stir just till mixed. Stir in nuts.

Grease and flour 8½x4½x2½-inch loaf pan; pour in batter. Bake at 325° for 55 to 60 minutes. Cool 10 minutes, turn out of pan. For best flavor, store at least a day.

Iced Almonds

Heat 1 cup whole blanched almonds, ½ cup sugar, and 2 tablespoons butter in heavy skillet; stir till almonds are toasted, about 15 minutes. Stir in ½ teaspoon vanilla. Spread nuts on foil; sprinkle with ¾ teaspoon salt. Cool; break apart.

Keep glaze at *pouring* consistency while you ice Petits Fours—that's the secret for turning out a pretty candy-like finish.

Index